INTERNATIONAL C(

Published monthly, except July and August, by the
Carnegie Endowment for International Peace
Entered as second-class matter February 13, 1935, at the post office
at New York, N. Y., under the Act of March 3, 1879

AMERICAN FOREIGN TRADE POLICIES
By Cordell Hull

THE CONSEQUENCES OF ECONOMIC NATIONALISM
By Lionel Robbins

WORLD POLICE FOR WORLD PEACE
By Viscount Allenby

THE RESPONSIBILITY OF GOVERNMENTS AND PEOPLES
By Cordell Hull

EUROPE AT THE CROSSROADS
By Kamil Krofta

AMERICAN FOREIGN RELATIONS
By Cordell Hull

FRANCE FAITHFUL TO DEMOCRACY
By Léon Blum

OCTOBER, 1936
No. 323

CARNEGIE ENDOWMENT FOR INTERNATIONAL PEACE
DIVISION OF INTERCOURSE AND EDUCATION
PUBLICATION AND EDITORIAL OFFICES:
405 WEST 117TH STREET, NEW YORK CITY

Subscription price 25 cents for one year, one dollar for five years
Single copies 5 cents

CARNEGIE ENDOWMENT FOR INTERNATIONAL PEACE

Offices

700 Jackson Place, Washington, D.C.
405 West 117th Street, New York, N.Y.

TRUSTEES

WALLACE McK. ALEXANDER
California

ARTHUR A. BALLANTINE
New York

DAVID P. BARROWS
California

WILLIAM MARSHALL BULLITT
Kentucky

NICHOLAS MURRAY BUTLER
New York

DANIEL K. CATLIN
Missouri

JOHN W. DAVIS
New York

NORMAN H. DAVIS
New York

FREDERIC A. DELANO
District of Columbia

AUSTEN G. FOX
Rhode Island

FRANCIS P. GAINES
Virginia

CHARLES S. HAMLIN
Massachusetts

HOWARD HEINZ
Pennsylvania

ALANSON B. HOUGHTON
New York

FRANK O. LOWDEN
Illinois

PETER MOLYNEAUX
Texas

ANDREW J. MONTAGUE
Virginia

ROLAND S. MORRIS
Pennsylvania

HENRY S. PRITCHETT
California

ELIHU ROOT
New York

EDWARD LARNED RYERSON, JR.
Illinois

JAMES BROWN SCOTT
District of Columbia

JAMES R. SHEFFIELD
New York

MAURICE S. SHERMAN
Connecticut

JAMES T. SHOTWELL
New York

SILAS H. STRAWN
Illinois

ROBERT A. TAFT
Ohio

THOMAS JOHN WATSON
New York

DIVISION OF INTERCOURSE AND EDUCATION

Director, NICHOLAS MURRAY BUTLER

Office, 405 West 117th Street, New York, N.Y.
Telephone, University 4-1850—*Cable*, Interpax, New York

LE CENTRE EUROPÉEN
COMITÉ

RAFAEL ALTAMIRA Y CREVEA
Spain

MORITZ J. BONN
Germany

GUILLAUME FATIO
Switzerland

E. HELDRING
Netherlands

ANDRÉ HONNORAT
France

GEORGES LECHARTIER
France

HENRI LICHTENBERGER
France

COUNT A. VON MENSDORFF
Austria

MARQUIS PIERO MISCIATTELLI
Italy

GILBERT MURRAY
Great Britain

ALFRED NERINCX
Belgium

NICOLAS S. POLITIS
Greece

E. VON PRITTWITZ UND GAFFRON
Germany

JOSEPH REDLICH
Austria

COUNT CARLO SFORZA
Italy

J. A. SPENDER
Great Britain

COUNT PAUL TELEKI
Hungary

DR. BO ÖSTEN UNDÉN
Sweden

Directeur-Adjoint, MALCOLM W. DAVIS

Bureau, 173, Boulevard St.-Germain, Paris, France
Téléphone, Littré 88.50
Adresse Télégraphique, Interpax, Paris

ADVISORY COUNCIL IN GREAT BRITAIN

Sir Alan Anderson	Sir Frank Heath
Ernest Barker	Francis W. Hirst
Viscount Cecil of Chelwood	Lord Howard of Penrith
William P. Crozier	Herbert S. Morrison
Mrs. Mary Agnes Hamilton	Harold Temperley

Honorary Members, Gilbert Murray
J. A. Spender

Honorary Secretary, Mrs. Neville Lawrence

LONDON OFFICE

Representative in the United Kingdom, Hubert J. Howard
Address, 335, Abbey House, Victoria Street, S.W.1
Telephone, Abbey 7228
Cable, Carintpax, London

CONTENTS

	Page
Preface	451
American Foreign Trade Policies, by Cordell Hull	453
The Consequences of Economic Nationalism, by Lionel Robbins	466
World Police for World Peace, by Viscount Allenby	479
The Responsibility of Governments and Peoples, by Cordell Hull	487
Europe at the Crossroads, by Kamil Krofta	491
American Foreign Relations, by Cordell Hull	515
France Faithful to Democracy, by Léon Blum	524

PREFACE

The judgment of leading statesmen and scholars on some of the most vital of present-day problems are here placed before the readers of *International Conciliation*.

In the first article, which is the text of an address on the foreign trade policy of the United States delivered by the Honorable Cordell Hull, Secretary of State of the United States, before the general session of the twenty-fourth annual meeting of the Chamber of Commerce of the United States at Washington, D. C., last April, the process of negotiating the reciprocal trade agreements is explained with marked simplicity and clarity.

This is followed by a brief analysis of the causes, nature, and consequences of economic nationalism by Lionel Robbins, Professor of Economics in the University of London.

The third article, entitled "World Police for World Peace," is the text of the outstanding address made on April 28 last by Field-Marshal the Rt. Hon. Viscount Allenby as Rector of Edinburgh University. This was the last speech made by Lord Allenby before his death on May 14.

Secretary of State Hull's address to the World Power Conference at Washington on September 7, stressing the fact that the maintenance of peace in the world is the responsibility of governments and peoples alike, and the address by Mr. Hull dealing with international relations and international agreements, delivered in New York on September 15 before the Good Neighbor League, are also included.

In addition the pamphlet contains the speech on foreign affairs made by Dr. Kamil Krofta, Minister of Foreign Affairs of Czechoslovakia, on May 28, which is devoted in part to a review of the efforts made by various groups in Central Europe to solve their economic difficulties by means of regional agreements, and the text of Premier Léon Blum's brilliant speech in defense of the democratic system, broadcast from Paris on September 17.

Nicholas Murray Butler

New York, September 18, 1936.

AMERICAN FOREIGN TRADE POLICIES[1]

By the Honorable Cordell Hull
Secretary of State of the United States

One year ago, when I had the pleasure of addressing the general session of your twenty-third annual meeting,[2] I took occasion to lay before you the basic ideas which underlie the foreign commercial policy pursued by the Government of the United States during the gravest economic emergency within our peacetime experience. I described to you the pressing needs of this country and of the world in the domain of international commercial relations; the difficulties that stand in the way of meeting these needs; and the dangers which are inherent in failure to solve the vital problems involved. The twelve months that have elapsed have brought these needs and problems into still sharper relief, and in speaking before you today I welcome the opportunity to discuss with you once more, especially in the light of the developments and experience of the past eventful year, the purposes and objectives sought by our Government in the field of foreign trade.

As time goes on, it becomes increasingly clear that no nation can achieve a full measure of stable economic recovery so long as international trade remains in the state of collapse into which it was plunged during the years of the depression. The whole post-war period has been characterized by an ever-increasing drift toward economic nationalism, which has expressed itself in a constant growth of barriers to international trade. This drift has become enormously intensified during the past six years, though responsible statesmen in many countries have never ceased to deplore it. Under its impact the international economic structure of the world has been all but shattered, and individual nations have sought economic improvement more and more by means of purely domestic measures, on the basis of a greater degree of self-containment than was ever before consciously attempted.

Such a movement toward national economic self-containment is incompatible with the re-establishment of satisfactory prosperity.

[1] Address delivered before the general session of the twenty-fourth annual meeting of the Chamber of Commerce of the United States, Washington, D. C., April 30, 1936. Reprinted by permission from Publications of the Department of State, No. 875, 1936.
[2] *The Foreign Commercial Policy of the United States*, Publications of the Department of State, No. 733, 1935.

The basic raw materials needed for modern ways of living and for the development of a higher civilization in the future are not evenly distributed throughout the globe. Similarly, the application of technical skill and the accumulation of financial wealth are more highly developed in some nations than in others. No nation, forced to live in isolation within its own borders, can have everything that it needs. Overabundance of some resources cannot possibly compensate for lack or insufficiency of others. Only through international trade and financial intercourse can locally concentrated natural and man-made resources be utilized in such a way as to afford all nations the indispensable foundations of modern economic well-being.

For generations humanity has built its life upon a recognition of the primary fact that trade is the lifeblood of economic activity. This is equally true whether within or among nations. Each nation has accordingly developed far beyond domestic requirements those branches of production in which it has special endowment or aptitude. Each nation has come to regard foreign markets as the natural outlets for its surplus output, and the surplus production of other nations as the sources from which to supply its own deficiencies.

A rapid and drastic contraction of international trade of the kind that the world has witnessed during the past few years constitutes a double attack upon the economic well-being of each nation's population. The necessary materials habitually obtained in other parts of the globe become more difficult to secure. The surplus national production habitually shipped to other countries becomes more difficult to sell. Output in the surplus-creating branches of production must be curtailed, or else accumulating surpluses force prices below the level of remunerative return to the producers. In either case, the whole economic structure becomes disrupted. Vast unemployment ensues, not only in the field of production, but also in such lines of activity as transportation, banking, merchandising, and the various avocations and professions. Financial investment and other forms of savings become impaired or are wholly destroyed. Distress spreads throughout the nation in ever-widening circles.

Economic distress quickly translates itself into social instability and political unrest. It opens the way for the demagogue and the agitator, foments internal strife, and frequently leads to the supplanting of orderly democratic government by tyrannical dictatorships. It breeds international friction, fear, envy, and resentment, and destroys the very foundations of world peace. Nations are tempted to seek escape from distress at home in military adventures beyond their frontiers. And as fear of armed conflict spreads, even peace-loving nations are forced to divert their national effort from the creation of wealth and from peaceful well-being to the construction of armaments. Each step in the armament race bristles with new menace of economic disorganization and destruction, multiplies fear for the future, dislocates normal constructive processes of economic life, and leads to greater and greater impoverishment of the world's population.

In the past few months we have witnessed a swift increase in international political tension; a recrudescence of the military spirit which sees no goal in life except triumph by force; an expansion of standing armies; a sharp increase of military budgets; and actual warfare in some portions of the globe. Human and material resources are being shifted, on a truly alarming scale, in a military direction rather than in one of peace and peaceful pursuits.

There is no need for me to dwell long upon the appalling implications of this tragic picture. Overwhelming evidence of it is startlingly apparent on every side. I shall rather devote the time which you have so kindly placed at my disposal to a consideration of the possibilities of turning back this rising danger of a new world catastrophe. For myself, I am firmly convinced that such possibilities exist, and that the world has at its disposal adequate remedies for overcoming the virulent disease which is now so widespread.

Only as the world's economic health is restored will individuals and nations develop again adequate resistance to the psychological madness that makes possible internal and external strife. Only as constructive economic effort once more fully engages the energies of mankind, as the machinery of production and distribution regains and expands its scale and speed of operation, as sterile unemployment is replaced by fertile toil, will the nations of the world restore and develop their economic prosperity in full and sound measure and turn their thoughts away from war and toward lasting peace.

The disease is so widespread and so all-pervasive that the attack upon it must be on a wide front. In addition to the break-down of international trade, the economic life of each nation is subjected today to the strain of many maladjustments, both internal and external. Each of the major maladjustments must be corrected, for there is little hope of adequate and stable recovery if any of the more important ones are ignored or neglected.

Many of these maladjustments can yield only to constructive domestic measures, and such measures, looking especially toward the fullest practicable development of the domestic economy, are therefore indispensable to recovery. They are being taken today in many countries. But they cannot be really and permanently effective unless they go hand in hand with appropriate action in the international field. The prospect of full and durable recovery will be bright and hopeful only as each important nation determines to go forward both on a domestic and on an international program, in order that an expanding world prosperity may develop to sustain and promote the expansion of domestic recovery.

We in the United States are engaged today upon such a combined economic program. Under the influence of constructive internal measures, we have achieved a substantial recovery in production, employment, and prices. But we are also buttressing this developing economic improvement by a determined effort to re-establish international trade upon a basis that will permit it to regain its volume of a few years ago and to go forward as a process mutually beneficial to all nations.

At the time I addressed you a year ago, our foreign trade program was still in its beginnings. Since then it has developed into what we, who are daily engaged upon the task of its execution, believe to be an accomplishment of importance and increasing promise. We have now concluded twelve trade agreements, which have opened to larger American exports such markets as those of Canada, Cuba, Brazil, the Netherlands, Belgium, Sweden, and Switzerland.

In the process of preparing and negotiating these agreements, we have been confronted with the need of deciding many questions of method and of policy. If you will bear with me for a few minutes, I should like to describe to you briefly the methods we are employing for the attainment of our objectives, the decisions we have had to make in formulating our policy, and the reasons for choosing the particular methods and decisions.

The foreign-trade program of this Government is based fundamentally upon what to us is an indisputable assumption—namely, that our domestic recovery can be neither complete nor durable unless our surplus-creating branches of production succeed in regaining at least a substantial portion of their lost foreign markets. Our production of cotton, lard, tobacco, fruits, copper, petroleum products, automobiles, machinery, electrical and office appliances, and a host of other specialties is geared to a scale of operation the output of which exceeds domestic consumption by ten to fifty per cent. In his message to Congress recommending the passage of the Trade Agreements Act, the President urged the need of restoring foreign markets in order that our surplus-producing industries may be "spared in part, at least, the heart-breaking readjustments that must be necessary if the shrinkage of American foreign commerce remains permanent."

Our exports have shrunk for many reasons, among which two stand out prominently, both because of their effectiveness in reducing the volume of trade and because their removal or mitigation lies within the realm of possible action on our part. These are, first, the increase of trade barriers in those countries which constitute the normal markets for our exports, and second, the development of discriminatory practices on the part of such countries, which place our exporters at a disadvantage with respect to their foreign competitors.

Our needs are clear: we must induce foreign countries to mitigate the obstructions which they place in the way of our shipments to their markets, and we must free our export trade from disruptive discrimination directed against it. In what ways and by what means can we provide for these needs?

As regards the problem of trade barriers, it is not necessary for me to recite how, in recent years, customs duties have been raised to unprecedented heights in nearly all the countries of the world, nor how the use of new, powerfully restrictive devices has become widespread. You, as businessmen, are fully as familiar as I am with the operation of these measures and with their stifling effect upon the exchange of goods among the nations of the world. Nor is it necessary for me to emphasize the fact that our own country has contributed greatly to the rise of these barriers to trade.

Since the end of the World War, we have revised our general tariff structure upward on three different occasions. The third and most drastic of these revisions, embodied in the Smoot-Hawley Tariff Act, occurred at the very outset of the depression, from the devastating effects of which the world is just beginning to recover. Through that ill-starred action, we helped to set into motion a vicious spiral of retaliation and counterretaliation, and to start a race for a forcible contraction of international trade on a stupendous scale. In this race some nations have far outstripped us in the scope and effectiveness of restrictive action. Our export trade has become the victim of the formidable array of economic armament created by other nations, just as the export trade of other nations has likewise become the victim of our thrust into the heights of superprotectionism.

If international trade is to function again on an adequate scale, and if we are to regain our fair share of that trade, the nations of the world must retrace their steps from this supreme folly. As I said at the London Economic Conference in 1933, the nations, in the matter of tariffs, must embark upon a sound middle course between extreme economic internationalism and extreme economic nationalism. All excesses in the matter of trade barriers should be removed, and all unfair trade methods and practices should be abandoned.

When we were formulating our basic policy, there were two ways open to us to make our vital contribution to the process of economic demobilization. We could undertake a downward revision of our tariff by unilateral and autonomous action, in the hope that other nations would, as a result, also begin to move away from their present suicidal policies in the field of foreign trade. Or else we could, by the negotiation of bilateral trade agreements, attempt a mitigation of trade barriers on a reciprocal basis.

We chose the second course as offering by far the better promise of trade improvement. An autonomous reduction of our tariff would provide no assurance that our example would be followed by other nations or, if it would be followed, that the resulting mitigation of trade barriers would, in fact, apply to those commodities which are of the greatest interest to us. On the other hand, the bilateral method, combined with the principle of equality of treatment which I shall presently discuss, contemplates simultaneous action by many countries and, in its effects, operates to drive down excessive trade barriers throughout the world. Moreover, it affords us an opportunity to secure in each country the relaxation of restrictions with respect to those of our export commodities the sale of which in that country's markets is either of special importance to us or else has been particularly hard-hit by recently established restrictions. It was in order to make possible the securing of such concessions for our export trade by negotiation with other countries that Congress empowered the President, for a three-year period, to conclude reciprocal trade agreements and, in connection with such agreements, to modify, within strictly defined limits, customs duties and other import restrictions operative in the United States.

The process of negotiating foreign trade agreements of this type involves a task of enormous difficulty and complexity. In carrying it out, all appropriate divisions of the Government participate in a series of interdepartmental committees, and thus bring to bear upon the problem their specialized knowledge and judgment.

In addition, the Government seeks the fullest cooperation of the business community and the general public. Any interested person is given full opportunity to present his views to the interdepartmental Committee for Reciprocity Information. In the case of the countries with whom negotiations have been announced, approximately 2,500 briefs and statements have been submitted by interested firms and trade associations. These statements, as well as transcripts of the oral testimony presented to the Committee for Reciprocity Information, are placed in the hands of all the officials of the Government concerned with the preparation and negotiation of trade agreements. They are given careful study and constitute an important part of the material upon which decisions with respect to the requesting or granting of concessions are based.

In entering upon preparatory work with respect to any particular country, the experts of the interdepartmental organization of which I spoke a moment ago endeavor to obtain, first of all, a picture, as comprehensive as possible, of the trade relations existing between the United States and the other country. As regards our exports to the country with which negotiations are in progress, the experts make a thorough study of each commodity from the point of view of the customs treatment which it is accorded in that country.

All this and a great deal of other information is embodied in reports dealing with the commodities under review. Together with the representations made through the Committee for Reciprocity Information, the reports constitute the foundation upon which the decision is made as to what sort of concessions we should seek from the other country as regards duties, quotas, exchange controls, and other trade-obstructing devices. A schedule is then made up, comprising our requests, and is presented to the government of the other country for its consideration.

At the same time the representatives of the other country transmit to our Government a schedule of concessions which they would like to receive from us. These requests are immediately subjected to a close scrutiny by the experts of our Government comprising the interdepartmental organization. Previously to that, these experts had already made a thorough investigation of the principal commodities imported into the United States from the other country, and they are, therefore, prepared to give early and thorough consideration to the requests made by the other country.

In connection with each request, an examination is made of our recent tariff treatment of that commodity; of the status and development of the domestic production of that or similar commodities; of the competitive factors operating as between our domestic production and the production, not only in the country with which we are negotiating, but in all other countries which are actual or potential suppliers of the same commodity; of the effects—so far as they can be determined—of the present customs treatment upon trade in the particular commodity; of the probable effects of any change in the existing tariff rates; and of many other factors. The influence of possible tariff changes upon both producers and consumers in the United States is given careful consideration.

After all these studies are completed by our Government and the government of the other country, the negotiators come together, and the process of adjusting differences begins. It is inevitable, of course, that some differences of view are bound to exist and that many features of the schedule originally exchanged should become modified and adjusted.

The general aim of our negotiators is to secure concessions for those American exports the marketing of which in the other country offers the best opportunity of development and, at·the same time, promises the greatest degree of revival in our export industries; and to grant the other country concessions with respect to commodities the possible increased importation of which would be beneficial to our country. The representatives of the other country are, naturally, actuated by very much the same motives. In the actual experience of negotiation, it has been found possible to reconcile the desires of both sides in sufficient measure for the final agreements to embody worth-while mutual concessions and thus open the way for an increase of mutually profitable trade.

Our officials who are concerned with carrying out this complicated process of preparation and negotiation are actuated by only one purpose: to administer the Trade Agreements Act cautiously, conservatively, and practically, with the best interests of the country as a whole as their sole guide, and thus to carry out, scrupulously and accurately, the instructions and policy of Congress within the limits prescribed in the act. They are free, so far as is humanly possible, from partisan considerations. I do not know the politics of most of the persons engaged in this important task. I only know that some of them have had a long experience in practical business affairs, that some of them have devoted their lives to the study of industry, or agriculture, or trade, or tariffs, or economics in general. I know that each agreement, forged by their combined effort, represents an effective instrument for reopening the channels of international trade on an economic and constructive basis.

Unlike a general revision of the tariff, when Members of Congress are expected to read and digest, usually within a few weeks, many volumes of testimony and to determine how to vote on thousands of rates and classifications, each trade agreement requires the adjustment of a relatively small number of rates. These adjustments are made on the basis of tireless and earnest investigation, of constant checking and rechecking of all essential considerations, by the ablest and most practical and disinterested experts in trade and tariff matters that the State, Treasury, Agriculture, and Commerce Departments and the Tariff Commission can secure.

These men must, of necessity, work some of the time in executive session, just as committees of Congress do when the task of tariff revision is undertaken. Congressional tariff acts are usually drafted, in all their essentials, in such executive sessions, behind closed doors. Both political parties in Congress have almost invariably pursued this practice, for the purpose of necessary deliberation as well as in self-defense from day-and-night importunities of outsiders. Who would today attempt to label this a star-chamber procedure? Yet there are those who would carelessly apply this epithet to this identical method when practiced in connection with the negotiation of trade agreements. It must be clear to such critics that we have adopted our method on the basis of the long experience of Congress in dealing with questions of this type. It is with Congress, therefore, rather than with us, that necessity of the executive-session practice should be debated.

I come now to our second primary need in the field of foreign commerce—the freeing and safeguarding of our export trade from adverse discrimination on the part of foreign nations. It is clear that the mere mitigation of the tariff, quota, and other burdensome obstructions to our trade is not sufficient to enable us to regain our foreign markets; it is also necessary that the customs treatment accorded to our goods in each such market be at least as favorable as that accorded to the goods of our foreign competitors. In recent years our trade has suffered greatly because some of our competitors have secured, in many of our most important markets, exclusive advantages which have resulted in serious discrimination against us.

We could have embarked upon a similar line of policy. We, too, could have attempted to negotiate arrangements embodying exclusive advantages for our export trade. But it was clear to us from the outset that such a policy would have provided but a precarious safeguard for our trade. It would merely have served as an incentive for each of our competitors to seek further exclusive advantages, which would have immediately set up new discriminations against our trade—to be overcome by us in turn by means of new negotiations.

Generations of experience with various forms of international commercial relations have demonstrated fully that only the policy of equal treatment can secure for a nation stability of its international trade and freedom from disruptive discrimination, and that such a policy can operate only on the basis of the unconditional most-favored-nation principle. Only if the foreign country with which we enter into a trade agreement assures us the benefit of that principle can we be certain that our exports to that country's market will be able to compete with similar goods coming from other foreign countries on an equal footing, since under the most-favored-nation principle each advantage or concession granted to any other country would immediately and automatically be extended to us.

But if we were to ask of other countries a condition of complete equality for our trade—and, in justice to ourselves, we could accept nothing less—we could clearly offer other nations only a similar kind of treatment. Each exclusive concession granted by us to a foreign country would have constituted an immediate discrimination against fifty or more other countries. It would have involved us in constant negotiation and renegotiation, and would have given rise to retaliation abroad and continuing uncertainty for our business interests engaged in foreign trade. Hence, a provision was written into the Trade Agreements Act directing the President to generalize the duty adjustments effected through any trade agreement to goods coming from other countries, except those which discriminate against our trade or pursue other policies likely to defeat the aims which we seek to accomplish through the act.

Our trade-agreements program is thus a standing offer to all the nations of the world to deal with each of them in commercial matters on a basis of equal treatment. In carrying out the mandate of Congress in this respect, we have, save only in the case of a few well-recognized exceptions, steadfastly refrained from securing or granting preferential or discriminatory treatment. In generalizing the duty reductions negotiated in the individual trade agreements, we have sought to place on an equal footing those nations which, in turn, extend equality of treatment to our commerce, and to refuse such equality to those nations which refuse equality to us. Thus all phases of our policy are on a reciprocal basis.

Here again, as in the adjustment of duties, we strive to carry out our policy cautiously, conservatively, and practically. Our rule is that the duty reductions granted to each individual country are restricted to those commodities of which the particular country is the chief supplier to the United States. If it should happen, however, that, under existing abnormal conditions, some other country at any later stage profits unduly from the benefit of the concession, we retain the right, when such contingency arises, to modify the original grant.

Our interpretation of the most-favored-nation principle is sufficiently flexible to permit the negotiation of multilateral trade arrangements. We welcome such arrangements, provided they have for their object the liberalization and promotion of international trade in general, rather than the creation of closed areas of special preference. At the Seventh International Conference of American States at Montevideo, I proposed an agreement designed to pave the way for such arrangements. This agreement, which is open to adhesion by all countries, has been ratified by our Government.

These and other practical exceptions and safeguards, which existing abnormal conditions render necessary, in no way detract from the force and importance of the unconditional most-favored-nation principle as the foundation of the rule of equality of treatment in international commercial relations. Discrimination and preference can only result in a diversion of trade from channels of economic benefit to channels of political influence, and can provide but a weak and unsatisfactory basis for a restricted trade that is constantly at the mercy of political chance and change. Equality of treatment broadens and hastens the process of reduction of trade barriers. It offers the best general basis for restoring and expanding trade as an economically sound and universally beneficial process.

The firm determination on the part of the Government of the United States to reassert the rule of equality of treatment has already gone far to slow down the world's recent drift toward the chaos of discrimination and special advantage. We are doing everything in our power, through the trade-agreements program and through other channels of influence open to us, to induce the other great trading nations of the world to adopt a similar attitude toward the problem of rehabilitation of world trade. In such rehabilitation lies the greatest single hope that the world may still be spared the tragedy of another destructive upheaval.

In brief, through our present foreign-trade program, we are attempting to increase trade by a mitigation of existing trade barriers and to restore trade to its accustomed economic channels by the reestablishment of the rule of equality of treatment in commercial relations. This twofold endeavor is directed, first and foremost, toward overcoming the emergency conditions which have resulted in drastic contraction and diversion of trade. The Trade Agreements Act is a temporary measure which was enacted primarily for the purpose of enabling us to deal effectively with this acute emergency.

Although experience has already demonstrated that, under existing circumstances, the negotiation of reciprocal trade agreements represents the only constructive approach, in the field of commerce, to the problem of broad and sound economic recovery, there are some in this country who, without waiting for the economic emergency to be brought under control, demand the immediate repeal of the act and the abandonment of the trade agreements negotiated under its authority. Let us face squarely what that would mean. We would automatically go back to the Smoot-Hawley tariff and face once more the vicious discrimination against our trade which it caused and the virtually suicidal effort at economic self-containment which it represented. This futile and fatal course backward would involve a steadily increasing aggravation of regulation and regimentation in our economic life. Yet some of those who voice loudest their opposition to regimentation in general demand, at the same time, a commercial policy that would inevitably lead to such regimentation, and to a permanently increasing dole as well.

This is the real alternative to our present course of action. It would represent an inglorious surrender to the emergency that has overwhelmed us. Far from overcoming that emergency, it would deepen and widen the ravages of the maladjustments that constitute the very foundation of our present economic difficulties, and of the existing threat to world peace. Our program, on the other hand, holds increasing promise of success in dealing with the grave exigency that confronts us at this time.

Through its trade-agreements program, this country is furnishing its fair share of leadership in the world movement toward a restoration of mutually profitable international trade and, as a consequence, toward an improvement in the employment of labor, a fuller measure of stable domestic prosperity, and the only sound foundation for world peace. And we, who are concerned with the execution of the program, find special gratification in the fact that our effort in this direction has widespread support in the nation as a whole. The press of this country, in its vast majority, has been clear-sighted enough to recognize the vital importance of the program. Great business organizations, like yours, have given us invaluable encouragement. With such inspiration to guide us, we shall go forward in our effort to bring peace and prosperity out of political tension and economic distress.

THE CONSEQUENCES OF ECONOMIC NATIONALISM[3]

By Lionel Robbins
Professor of Economics in the University of London

I

One of the most marked characteristics of the present state of trade is the extent to which recovery is limited to the home market. Save in the countries still on gold at the old parity, there has been considerable improvement all over the world. But except in so far as domestic revival has involved an increase in demand for essential raw materials from abroad, as in the case of the British building boom, world trade has lagged far behind this recovery. International investment has virtually ceased. The great ports are working far below capacity. Shipping is still in a position of great difficulty. The export industries of this and many other countries still enjoy the status of depressed areas.

The causes of all this are by no means simple. The great fall in raw material prices has been such as especially to affect the capacity of many countries to purchase imports. The failure of the investments of the twenties has created great distrust of international lending. Structural changes have curtailed demand for what were at one time staples of trade. But over and above all these influences, which in greater or less degree have their precedents in earlier depressions, certain forces are operative tending to a permanent contraction of international business, the forces of economic nationalism. It is the purpose of this paper to attempt to analyze briefly the nature of these forces and to discuss their general economic and political significance.

II

It is the essence of economic nationalism that it attempts to confine business activities which would otherwise be international to the area of the political unit. The detailed manifestations are various. They range from the simple protective tariff on the one hand to the most thorough-going socialist planning on the other. But they all have this characteristic in common—the tendency to self-sufficiency. It is irrelevant, so far as their effects are concerned, whether

[3] Reprinted by permission from the May, 1935, issue of the *Monthly Review* of Lloyds Bank Limited, London, E. C. 3.

they spring from a desire for military security, or from the desire to preserve certain industries, or from the desire to exercise detailed control over the whole mechanism of economic life within the area of State sovereignty. The nature of economic nationalism is independent of its causes.

Now it is obvious that economic nationalism is not new. Protective tariffs are much older than the conditions of freedom which, in some countries for a brief epoch, superseded them. In Great Britain central control of investment, however mild, is still sufficiently new to be resented, if not actively resisted. But elsewhere it has been fairly common. Control of migration is certainly no novelty: men have seldom been free to go where they wished. And throughout history somewhere or other the authorities of national States have been practicing that particular form of economic nationalism which is monetary depreciation or debasement. There are precedents for almost all the measures which are now affecting the prosperity of world trade.

What is new in the present situation is not the nature of the measures now prevalent but the extent of the area over which they are practiced. Tariffs we have always had with us. But we have never had tariffs of the magnitude of the systems now in vogue. Quantitative controls may here and there have made their appearance, but never, in modern times, have we had such a proliferation of quotas and license schemes over such a wide extent of trade. There have been monetary depreciations, but never during times of peace has the monetary unity of the world been so seriously disrupted. And the control of investment and migration has reached dimensions unprecedented since the beginning of the money economy.

But all this is no accident. It is really very superficial to put it all down to the depression. No doubt many of the restrictions from which trade is at present suffering are the hasty measures of governments made desperate by the ravages of the depression and the instability of the exchanges; there is indeed a vicious circle in these matters. But, on a wider view, the depression itself is in part at least a product of the growing restriction of trade and the divergent tendencies of national policies. There were business fluctuations long before economic nationalism became acute; if there had been no economic nationalism in the twenties there would still have been ups and downs of trade. But the course of depression in a world free from the restrictions of the post-war period would have been radically different from the depression we have known.

Some of these measures are due to fear of war, some to the growth of socialism, some merely to the influence of vested interests. But, quite apart from the initiating cause, the fact is that there is a sort of snowball principle about them all, which, once a certain point has been reached, necessarily involves what is virtually a transformation of the whole framework of economic activity. For a long time tariffs may continue to grow without causing much dislocation. But sooner or later the tariff as such becomes inadequate and gives way to more effective measures, the quota and the license system. For a long time small controls may be imposed on the machinery of investment. But there comes a time when control, to be effective, must be carried much further. Effectively to keep capital at home, not only the machinery of new issues but the stock markets and the foreign exchanges must be controlled. Similarly with money; for a time it is possible to make small departures from the international trend within the framework of a world system. But, beyond a certain point, the attempt to run with the hare and hunt with the hounds breaks down. It is a case for thorough-going nationalism or a return to an international system.

All this of course is what is happening before our eyes at the present day. The vast reversal of the tendency towards internationalism, which began far back in the seventies with the German revolt against free trade, slowly gathered way before the war, was greatly accelerated during that disaster, and since then has grown with such rapidity that it is no exaggeration but a calm statement of fact to say that it is today radically changing the system under which we live. This may sound strong to the inhabitants of Anglo-Saxon countries; so far we have been fortunate: we started late and we have great resources. But we have only to cast our gaze across the channel to see more advanced examples of the same tendency. Dr. Schacht's planned economy seems still very alien to our way of thinking, but so much has been done in the last period of bad trade that it would be foolish to be over-confident that still more may not be done in the next. Nationalism in one part breeds nationalism in others. If there is not a great reversal of the trend of policy the next depression may see even Great Britain many stages nearer the autarchistic plan.

III

But will this matter very much? Ought we to deplore this tendency to a break-up of the world economy? May it not be that the belief in free international intercourse is another of those nineteenth century shibboleths which all enlightened men must discard? Certainly no social arrangement can be regarded as sacrosanct nowadays. Before we conclude that a curtailment of international economic relations is an evil we must know exactly what it involves.

Let us start with simple protectionism, whether by way of tariffs or quantitative control of imports. It should not be difficult to see that, in the vast majority of cases, this involves a sacrifice of real income, both in the country imposing the obstacle and in the countries affected. If in the absence of protection it would pay to get things from abroad rather than produce them at home, this means that they can be produced more cheaply abroad and that domestic capital and labor will produce more if put to other uses. If therefore international exchange is impeded, the goods which are now produced at home are produced less cheaply; there are fewer obtained from a given quantum of resources than would have been obtained by putting the same resources to other uses and if the goods in question were obtained by way of exchange. At the same time the foreign resources which would have produced the goods whose exchange is now impeded have to work at less productive margins. In short, there is less real income all round. The wrong goods are produced in the wrong places.

We can see this very clearly if we look at what is happening today in agricultural production. It is one of the important structural changes of our time. For various reasons, partly fear of war, partly in order to secure the support of the agrarian electorate, ever since the beginning of the twenties, the governments of Europe have been erecting higher and higher obstacles to agricultural imports. The result is a state of affairs which can only be described as fantastic. Behind the obstacles prices are fifty, one hundred, even two hundred per cent higher than those in the world market. In Germany there is even a shortage of essential goods such as butter. At the same time the great areas of the new world which have specialized in the production of these commodities, and which can obviously produce them at much less cost, are thrown into violent dislocation. What is a luxury in poverty-stricken Europe, is destroyed or sold at prices far below cost of production in areas which in turn are poverty-stricken because of the policy of Europe.

But things do not end here. These countries are indebted to the inhabitants of manufacturing areas. In order to procure foreign exchange to pay their debts, and in order to provide employment for their people, they impose tariffs and restrictions on the import of European manufactures. There are developing in these parts, behind artificial obstacles to trade, industries which would never have paid under free trade conditions. This in turn hits the manufacturing areas. Directly by way of import restriction, indirectly by way of the competition of new supplies, the manufacturers of Europe experience a falling-off of demand for their products. The payment of interest on debt is impeded. The flow of new investment diminishes almost to zero. And all this to render unnecessary those shifts of productive power to forms of production hitherto extra-marginal which science and the international division of labor now render possible!

It is sometimes urged that considerations of this sort apply only to agrarian protection. It is agreed that it is destructive of wealth to impose obstacles on the exchange of food or raw materials. But it is urged that the existence of modern machine technique renders international division of labor unnecessary in industrial manufacture. Industrial protection it is urged is relatively innocuous.

The argument is specious, but it does not bear examination. The case for international division of labor in industry, as in agriculture, rests on differences of cost. So long as the costs of production are different in different areas, so long will it be advantageous for each area to specialize in producing those things in which its costs of production are least and to procure the rest by way of exchange from elsewhere. These cost differences depend in the last analysis on the different relative scarcities of the different factors of production in different parts of the world—depend, that is to say, on differences of labor costs, rent charges, raw material prices, transport charges, etc. There is no presumption at all that modern technique renders any less essential nice attention to these matters. Indeed, quite the contrary. Is it really to be supposed that all the branch factories of the different international concerns, which are erected in order to get round the tariffs, would come into existence if the tariffs were not there? The economies of large-scale production rest on large markets, but, save in a few favored areas, the existence of national limitations render large markets impossible. The world would be a much richer place if markets were more extensive.

IV

But it is not only as regards the distribution of existing resources that economic nationalism leads to results which by most would be regarded as uneconomical. The distribution of new capital and the whole future development of world resources is also likely to be seriously affected.

Under conditions of free investment, capital flows to the point of maximum return, account being taken of variations of risk. This means that capital tends to flow from areas where it is relatively plentiful to areas where it is relatively scarce. Now in fact the different parts of the world are in very different stages of economic development. There is reason to suppose that, given peace, stable government and freedom of investment, for a very long time to come, capital would flow from those parts which are relatively rich to those parts which are relatively poor, to the enrichment of each. From the economic point of view, the world is still relatively undeveloped; and the prospects of increased wealth all round, which would follow better exploitation of its resources, are great.

But under economic nationalism, this process of development must inevitably be considerably limited. This is not merely a matter of the immense obstacle to international investment which is offered by that form of economic nationalism which involves instability of exchanges; the effects of that are too well known to need further mention here. It is rather the effect of economic nationalism as regards long-term investment. So long as the governments of areas where capital is relatively scarce are unwilling to see domestic resources controlled by foreign owners; so long as the authorities of the areas where capital is relatively plentiful impose hindrances on its movement elsewhere—and as economic nationalism grows this must come more and more to be the case—so long must this impoverishment of the world continue. There must be stagnation and ultra-cheap money in the capital exporting centers, financial stress and a chronic scarcity of capital in the centers which would have imported capital. Moreover—and this is a point which especially concerns Great Britain—the great export trades, which have been geared up, so to speak, to meet the demands created by a large export of capital, must remain permanently depressed. Not merely the business of acceptance and new issue, but the whole business of export suffers further from the stoppage of free capital movement.

It may be said that all this is hasty generalization from the difficulties of the moment, and that "when things get better"—it is never stated quite how—even under the régime of separate national planning we shall see a revival of orderly international borrowing and lending.

It is to be feared that the wish is father to the thought. For the probabilities are all in the other direction. The existence of national controls of the business of investment is likely to make the movement of capital not more, but very much less, considerable than would otherwise be the case. When one set of investors in one country lends to another set of borrowers elsewhere that is an affair of private business in which the intervention of governments is the exception rather than the rule. But when the investment board of one country lends to the investment board of another that is *ipso facto* a matter of high diplomacy involving political risks and considerations quite unconnected with the relative scarcity of capital in the countries concerned. It is really not to be expected that under such a régime the movement of capital would be on anything like the scale which might be expected in a régime of free private investment. The Russian credits are sometimes invoked as a demonstration that even under national socialism some borrowing takes place, but the example is surely very unconvincing. Who can doubt that if the revolution had taken a different form and there had been scope for free investment and private property in Russia that the volume of foreign investment in those parts since the war would have been incomparably greater? A world of economic nationalism is going to be a world in which the undeveloped areas are much less rapidly developed and at much greater cost than would be the case in a world of international cooperation. And the centers which in the past have grown up to organize the business of international investment must be doomed either to decline or to a very radical transformation of their business.

V

If the analysis of the preceding sections is correct, it seems that both in respect of the distribution of different industries in different parts of the world and in respect of the distribution of new capital investment, economic nationalism must lead to the loss of much potential wealth.

But is this necessarily to be regretted? May it not be that the sacrifice of potential wealth may be regarded as a fair price for the greater economic security and freedom from external development which the national control of national development and resources must involve? This at least is the argument of the more sophisticated advocates of economic nationalism.

Unfortunately these claims do not seem to be justified. If we could assume that economic nationalism would result in complete isolation of each national economy it might be that its effects would be limited to those we have already examined. It would be as if there had been a fragmentation of the planet along the lines of division indicated by the political maps. The inhabitants of each splinter would be deprived of resort to outside supplies in times of harvest shortage and the like, and their opportunities would be greatly restricted. But they would at least be immune from fluctuations generated outside their area. There would be no foreigner to blame for variations of prosperity.

Such developments, however, are not likely. The apparatus of modern life is so dependent on supplies of raw materials unequally distributed about the surface of the earth, that it is really most improbable that the majority of nations would be content with the very drastic alterations of habit which abstention from the consumption of all commodities dependent on import would involve. Moreover the countries especially dependent on export of such materials would no doubt make strong efforts to secure outlets for their wares even at some sacrifice of the principles of autarchy. The net effect, therefore, even of the very drastic economic nationalism which seems to lie ahead is likely to be a severe curtailment rather than a total cessation of international business. There will be some international exchange. But it will be much more a matter of bilateral treaties and special governmental bargains; much less a matter of world markets and competitive enterprise than heretofore.

But this does not mean that it will be more secure and more stable. On the contrary there is reason to believe that in such a régime there will exist types of instability and insecurity, which are much less frequent in a régime of free markets.

Consider, for instance, the determination of prices. In the world market this is a resultant of the impersonal impact of demand and supply from a multitude of sources. In the planned system it will be a matter of bilateral bargains. It will be much less a matter of consumers' wants and the technical means of satisfying them, much more a matter of political higgling. And it will be political higgling in the dark. There will be no world market to guide it. The world market with its "wasteful competition" and its "parasitical middlemen" will have disappeared. Under bilateral monopoly price is subject to very wide limits of error.

All this will be inconvenient, but it will be by no means the main inconvenience of such a régime. The system is designed to guard against change, but change cannot be thought out of the picture. There will be changes of technical knowledge in this part of the world or that, harvest variations, changes in the demand for and supply of various natural resources. And the effects of such changes are likely to be much more devastating in a world of economic nationalism than in a world of free markets. The damping effect of the world market will have gone. The safety valve of migration will have disappeared. The rigid system which remains will be much less capable of adaptation.

Consider the effects of some invention resulting in a curtailment of demand for a staple article of export of a single State or group of States. Suppose, for example, a change in building methods or methods of paper production involving a considerable diminution in demand for certain kinds of timber. Or suppose some chemical discovery superseding the demand for some natural fertilizer.

It is clear that in any case the transition would be difficult. In any case there would probably be some permanent lowering of the value of land in the areas affected. Unless some of the population were willing to migrate there would probably be a permanent lowering of the standard of living.

But compare the difficulties of adaptation under the two systems. In a free system some laborers would probably migrate, and some would turn their efforts to other lines of production. New products or additional supplies of products hitherto produced elsewhere would appear in world markets.

But in a world of economic nationalism how much harder would be the transition. There would be no outlet by way of migration; national planning precludes free migration. And the outlet for new products or additional supplies of products hitherto produced elsewhere would be hedged in all round by existing agreements and prohibitions. The "ruinous" competition of the new products of the impoverished area would be resisted on all sides. In the few markets to which they succeeded in gaining access, the lowering of price necessary to carry off the increased supplies would be much greater than would be the case if the area of sale were less circumscribed. If the original falling-off of demand were very great, it might well be that the impoverishment of the inhabitants of the affected area would be catastrophic.

The picture is alarming. But it is not wholly imaginary. If we reflect on the recent history of the world it is not difficult to find examples. The causes of the increase of Japanese competition in recent years are many and complex. But one at least of these causes was the falling-off of demand for Japanese silk in American markets. And one reason at least for the great severity of Japanese competition in the countries to which Japanese goods have access is the very considerable obstacles which have been erected to the importation of such goods elsewhere. No doubt there is much more in it than this. But the example is conducive to reflection. And, as we shall see, it has a further moral which is even more disturbing.

VI

It seems therefore as though the policy of economic nationalism were likely to lose the substance for the shadow, even in regard to security. If the policy is imitated elsewhere—and it is the most astounding naïveté to argue as if the policy can be restricted only to one's own national area—then insecurity is increased. It is not a question of bartering the prospects of increased wealth for increased security. Security goes as well.

All this relates only to the economic consequences of economic nationalism. Even more important and even more disturbing are the probable political consequences. There is reason to believe that economic nationalism is likely gravely to enhance the danger of war. The idea that the peace of the world is likely to be increased if we "try to keep ourselves to ourselves" is not merely a pathetic fallacy, it is a highly dangerous delusion.

We have had occasion to recognize already how economic nationalism necessarily leads to what may be called, to borrow a very ugly word from the home of modern economic nationalism—the *politicalization* (*politizierung*) of trade. Instead of the consignment of sardines from Utopia to Ruritania being a matter of trade between Utopian and Ruritanian merchants, it becomes a matter of diplomacy. The High Contracting Parties undertake to receive and deliver sardines! It is clear that if anything goes wrong it is much more likely to lead to political friction than when private merchants were the parties involved. The very terms of contract are matters of politics. One has only to consider the part played by bacon in our own relations with Denmark in recent years to see how relations which have hitherto been completely cordial may be worsened by contracts over humble articles of trade.

But the "politicalization" of trade is not the only, or indeed the chief, political danger of economic nationalism. The main danger is the worsening of relations between States of unequal natural resources and populations—the so-called "haves" and "have-nots" of popular discussion—which it almost certainly involves.

It is a commonplace of elementary economics, that *so long as trade and investment are free*, territorial possession is a matter of secondary importance. So long as territorial possession involves no discrimination against the foreigner, the fact of possession confers no major gain, its absence no important disadvantage. No doubt the possession of an empire does involve some economic advantage. It affords outlets for employment in government service—the one service for which recruitment is almost necessarily chiefly confined to citizens. It carries with it some sentimental and linguistic advantage in matters of contracts. But quantitatively, so long as trade is free, these things do not amount to much. If an empire is not run as a private preserve, its advantages, such as they are, are mainly political rather than economic. So long as Great Britain adhered to the policy of the "open door," it was no empty claim that those parts of the Empire which were administered from at home were administered as if in trust for the world. The myopic apostles of continental reaction, who never understood the principles of classical liberalism and whose minds were befuddled by the leaden clangor of another imperial idea, may have denied this. But their accusations do not hold water. The administration of the free trade Empire is not one of the episodes of history of which Englishmen need be ashamed. No foreigner was poorer because of the width of our possessions, so long as these principles were adhered to. If he said he was, he can only have been hoping that if his government possessed them, it would administer them on different principles.

But once the principles of economic nationalism hold sway, the position is changed completely. If national (or imperial) areas are to be treated as private property, their markets preserved for citizens of the group in question, their resources open only to development by national (or imperial) capital, then territorial possession does matter very much indeed. If such is the state of affairs, then it is true that those outside the charmed circle may be very seriously affected by decisions which are taken within it. It does mean that absence of territorial possession may be a very grave disadvantage. The claim for a place in the sun ceases to be empty bombast, it becomes the fateful expression of an urgent and insistent need.

Now this is a very serious matter—and the more fortunate an area is in its initial possessions the more probable the ultimate menace to its security. If it can truly be said by the leaders of a hungry people—"*your poverty is the result of their policy. Your deprivation is the result of their possession*"—then there is grave risk of war, there is real danger of a combination of the "have-nots" to plunder the "haves." The belief that in the past the origins of war have been chiefly economic is false. Examination of the facts does not bear it out. But in a world of exclusive nationalism it is likely to become a grim and horrible reality. In a liberal world the theory of the economic causation of war is a malignant invention. Economic nationalism creates the conditions which make it true.

It is important to be quite clear about the issues involved here. It is not, as is often supposed, a mere matter of the unequal distribution of mere sources of raw materials. Of course the warlike peoples would wish to own their raw material supplies. But this is a minor matter, and, war apart, it is not difficult to buy raw materials if you have the money. The core of the problem is exclusion from local markets, from the markets for goods, for capital, for labor. And it is not possible to conceive of a redistribution of possessions which would put this right. The well-meaning idealists who talk in terms of some spectacular sacrifice on the part of the "haves" which once and for all will satisfy the "have-nots" have got things all out of perspective. The thing is politically absurd and economically useless. What is needed is not the handing over to this or that dictator of a few hundred square miles of fertile land (or desert)—however grand that might seem to the people who do not inhabit the area sacrificed. What is needed is the lowering of all those barriers to trade and investment which give the dictators and others a real pretext for the argument that the accident of history which marked out their particular area was also an accident which doomed its inhabitants to avoidable poverty. Until that is done the danger of war will persist. It was not doctrinaire pedantry which made the great British statesmen of the nineteenth century free traders: it was a shrewd and solid conception of the peace and wellbeing of the Empire.

VII

Impoverishment, insecurity, war—these, if our argument is correct, are likely to be the fruits of economic nationalism. The argument is not a new one. It was well known to those who built up the strength and the wealth of our nation in the past. But in recent years we have been apt to dismiss it as academic and unimportant. May it not be hoped that the portentous demonstration of its validity which is now unfolding itself before our eyes may restore our conviction of its practical significance and importance? It is not too late even now to escape from our present muddle, if only we have the wish to do so. The important thing is that we should recognize that it is a muddle—and a dangerous muddle at that—and not the somewhat arduous pathway to some nebulous and vaguely superior El Dorado which current obscurantism would have us believe it.

WORLD POLICE FOR WORLD PEACE[1]

By FIELD-MARSHAL THE
RT. HON. VISCOUNT ALLENBY, G.C.B., G.C.M.G., G.C.V.O.

More than half a century ago I entered the Army; with little ambition, vague as to the future, accepting events as they came along. As I was without any military connections or army influence, I had no expectation or idea of attaining the rank of Field-Marshal. Further I never dreamt that your university might raise me to the dignity of a Doctor of Laws; that I should have the honor of receiving the Livingstone Gold Medal of the Royal Scottish Geographical Society; or—highest distinction of all—that I might be chosen by you as Rector of the University of Edinburgh.

All these things have come to pass.

Knowing that pride is a sin to be reprehended, while gratitude is commendable, I will not proclaim my pride; but I do express my heartfelt gratitude to all those who have helped me on my way through life, especially to you who have elected me for the exalted and honorable position in which I now stand.

As a mere soldier, I am diffident in addressing you, my fellow members; you who are superior to me in every branch of knowledge except perhaps the barren business of War—and, even in that, I am now no longer up to date; though still on the active list of the Army.

I am fully conscious of my limitations; but the situation must be accepted, the duty has to be faced; nothing was ever won by shirking an issue or shrinking from an obligation.

I have not had the good fortune to enjoy a university education, but I have been privileged to know men and women of intelligence and learning in all walks of life; and it has been my constant endeavor to profit by the association. In that effort I hope I have been successful. Moreover, I have always tried to keep my mind from stagnation; and in this I have been gratuitously aided by the system of continual inspection and frequent examination, by papers and word of mouth, which prevails in the Army and which no soldier—however unaspiring—is able to elude. Notwithstanding all that effort to preserve and stimulate our mental powers we soldiers are sometimes looked down on, as below the average educational standard; especially so, per-

[1] Rectorial address delivered at Edinburgh University, April 28, 1936. Reprinted from The New Commonwealth Institute Publications, Series B, No. 9, May, 1936, London, S. W. 1.

haps, cavalry men—of whom I am one. However, I assure you that your armed forces take their profession seriously; are as earnest, industrious, and competent as any equal number of civilians. We are interested in and we study each our own technical branch; while appreciating whole-heartedly and with admiration the zeal and efficiency of our brothers in arms belonging to the other units in the Service—here at home and throughout the Empire overseas—all bound with spontaneous loyalty to one another, under and in humble duty to His Majesty the King-Emperor.

But not only in the regular forces of the Crown is that sense of loyalty found. Linked thereby, united as one, the sons and daughters of the Empire when the supreme test of the Great War came were equal to every trial; they joined the national fighting and civil services, bore unmurmuringly the brunt, and emerged victorious; women, in heroism, rivalling—if not excelling—the men.

Since victory came, many years have rolled by. What has victory given us? How do we stand?

Some of our statesmen and leaders, enthusiastic and optimistic, as well as they might be, acclaimed the termination of hostilities as the glorious and welcome conclusion of a war which was to end all wars. The golden age had arrived, to stay with us eternally.

We have waited long. The golden promise has not yet materialized. Still, do not let us accept the belief that all our efforts were futile; that our sacrifices were offered in vain.

Truly, the fruit for which we hungered is not yet ripe for the gathering; but we were, perhaps, hasty and premature in expectation of reward; our disappointment may thus be the penalty of impatience, natural as that impatience might be and indeed was after relaxation from the long and almost intolerable strain.

During those terrible years, humanity was shocked and shaken to a degree without precedent; mentally and morally, we are still unbalanced. Furthermore, the loss of our best and bravest has stripped from the world the flower and pride of its youth. Not only does our own Empire thus suffer; it is the plaint of every land and people whom the Great War touched.

Those who today should have been in the prime of manhood, able and eager to join with brain, heart, and hand in the colossal task of reconstruction are gone; before their work as citizens could even begin.

But though we deplore their loss and miss their cooperation, we must not let ourselves be mastered by despair. The work has to be carried on; and it is for the present young generation—with broad outlook and liberal education—to undertake the rebuilding of a broken world.

To you, here, in this venerable center of universal knowledge is offered full opportunity of acquiring that breadth of outlook, and of assimilating the wisdom of ages past and present; to lay the foundation of a liberal education.

Foundation, I say; meaningly; because education is never complete, self-education should continue while life lasts.

It is on all of you who belong to the young and rising generation that the future of our civilization depends. You have got to fit yourselves, now, for the enterprise awaiting you. The responsibilities to be incurred will be heavy, but you dare not attempt to escape from them, they must be courageously undertaken and carried through with dogged determination. The labor, though severe, is honorable in the highest degree; yet, remember that you cannot expect recognition by personal honors bestowed; you will have to set about the work in a spirit of altruism, and the reward for your altruism will be the inwardly sure knowledge that so far as in you lies you have done your duty and have deserved success, even if success has not crowned your efforts.

During the protracted course of that grim period of international strife many deplorable acts were committed, even by civilized nations and Christian peoples; their sanguinary and fratricidal disputes involving, in the quarrel, communities of other faiths and of culture less advanced.

The prestige of the elder nations has been weakened thereby; for the more backward races see their would-be mentors fallen from the exalted moral standard which the mentors themselves erected.

It will require much time to undo the harm thus brought about; to recover the ground lost; but faith and firm resolve can remedy the evil; and it is worth doing, because otherwise the future holds for us no hope.

It should be recognized that human nature remains as it has ever been; kindly, on the whole, and well-disposed; faithful in friendship; manifesting admirable qualities of self-abnegation and of superb courage, in support of high ideals, or defense of kith and kin. Such qualities may—it is true—become distorted, in grave crises, as when national existence is at stake; and may become exaggerated and changed, till marked by ferocity and even cruelty, in extreme trial; but, war at an end, old hatreds may be expected to weaken and gradually to disappear, though persisting longer between communities than between individuals.

The pity of it is that progress towards reconciliation is hampered and retarded by the fact that after a lengthy period of general insanity, such as was experienced in the years 1914-1918 and which has not even now been completely cured, each nation has difficulty in recognizing recovery of reason by other nations; hence arise suspicion and distrust. Thus fear is bred; and fear is an evil counsellor; it produces nothing better than a narrow nationalism; nationalism disguised as—and mis-called—patriotism; but which is at bottom only selfish jealousy, and mutual suspicion.

Nationalism is commonly held up to admiration; praised as a high—perhaps the highest—virtue; while internationalism—which is, in other words, generous sympathy with our fellow men—is often branded as a crime, a surrender, a betrayal of our own peculiar interests and rights.

Until this view—this regrettable attitude—is altered, we cannot hope for any enduring amelioration in international relations. Let us adopt a broader view.

It is frequently said that war is in accordance with the law of nature; that man has always fought and always will fight, that human nature cannot be changed. As I have already suggested—human nature is not a bad nature; it need not be changed, but it can be trained and guided—by education and example—to its betterment.

From earliest days, in the evolution and rise of "Homo Sapiens," competition has always been bitter. From the beginning, he found it cruelly hard to live; the strong arm was law, and only the fittest won through to survival. Man fought man; then family fought family; families combined, for defense or aggression; tribes resulted from the association of the families, and held their own for awhile against tribes similarly formed; till, eventually, tribes joined forces; and nations came into being.

Nations now maintain internal peace and good order by means of their own organized police forces, who restrain personal and party brawling. But as yet there are no international police; and nations continue to make war on each other, freely, and look on it as a matter of course.

To an unprejudiced and dispassionate observer there can be, however, no obvious reason why the rational procedure which has resulted in the establishment of a happy social state by the fusion in amity of once hostile tribes should not be extended to the creation of a wide comity of nations, nations independent yet interdependent; a world federation or fellowship. The open hand concealing no weapon.

And, in the end, war is not a satisfactory method of settling disputes. Ordeal by battle brings lasting benefit to neither combatant.

What have availed the victories of Napoleon Bonaparte? Where are the permanent advantages resulting from the political and military combinations, the strategical triumphs, of Moltke and Bismarck?

Wars have been usually waged—in olden days—for the spoils of victory; increase of territory; acquisition of wealth; even glory to the victor. That lust for expansion is not yet quite dead; but the glory of conquest is departing; its gains are Dead Sea fruit; its legacy revengeful memories alone; hardening hearts, perpetuating anger, and leading on to the dreary round of renewed wars.

We earth-dwellers are prisoners on the planet, there is no way out; so since we cannot escape from the proximity of our neighbors, it is surely better to live with them as friends than as enemies.

I am told, on good authority, that our globe can support human life for another two thousand million years or more.

If the men of science are correct in their estimate, the Earth is still young; barely middle-aged; and mankind is in a very early stage of babyhood. What sort of creatures our remote descendants may be, in the World's old age, or under what conditions they will exist, we cannot even guess.

The old order changeth; the dragons of the prime have had their day; and, a thousand million years hence, evolution may have brought into being a type of humanity differing as widely from ourselves as the Deinotherium from the Dormouse.

But our interests lie in the problems of today; political, social, economic; all of immediate urgency; the near not the distant future is our instant concern, and we should concentrate on that before it is too late.

There is danger in delay, for it seems likely that, unless an effort in the right direction—a successful effort—is made soon, the present social system will crumble in ruin; and many now alive may witness the hideous wreck. Then will loom the dreadful menace of the dark ages; returning, darker, black, universal in scope, long-lasting.

At the present moment, many years after the close of the war which was to bring enduring peace to all, we find the cleverest brains everywhere busily experimenting with new inventions for facilitating slaughter; building more horrible engines of destruction, brewing more atrocious poisons, designing more monstrous methods of murdering their fellow men and women.

If war comes on us, the peaceful inhabitants of our so-called civilized communities—our women and children not excepted—will be as open to attack as the soldier in the field; for the convention that non-combatants are respected no longer obtains.

Recent progress in science has now given to the machine the mastery over man its maker. Until lately, politicians and statesmen —who are the authors and the initiators of war—could feel safe in their own homes surrounded by their families. That happy security will be theirs no longer.

The knowledge of this may perhaps bring to the statesman a warning sense of his responsibility. The choice lies with him. Will the hardness of his heart prevail; must the narrowness of his outlook persist until he is schooled by poison-gas and bomb; or will he some day call to mind the pact renouncing war as a solvent of differences; the pact, signed by sixty nations, but now forgotten or disregarded? Is it too much to believe that the human intellect is equal to the problem of designing a world State wherein neighbors can live without molestation; in collective security? It does not matter what the State is called; give it any name you please: League of Nations; Federated Nations; United States of the World. Why should there not be a *world* police; just as each nation has a national police force?

Many former obstacles have been cleared away. Science has overthrown barriers and given egress in all directions. Man is now able to navigate the atmosphere, plumb the deep seas, travel in three dimensions of space, move anywhere at a speed unimaginable to our fathers. Willingly or unwillingly, he has become a world-citizen; and the duties of that citizenship cannot be evaded; duties calling for the whole-hearted cooperation of every man and woman alive, joined in mind and purpose to promote the good and the advancement of all.

And machinery is ready to hand. The League of Nations is alive and active, while courts exist for determining and adjusting international differences, judicial and financial.

No nation, at heart, wants war; but in the course of history it has happened and is happening that ambitious leaders, inspired by a narrow nationalism, may exercise a compelling influence on impressionable and inexperienced youth to urge them on a path of promised glory. This, especially in countries which have suffered recent territorial loss or whose over-crowded population is looking for outlet, exerts a magnetic lure on immature minds.

Dictators are, however, but ephemeral phenomena; they do not represent the democracy, the sovereignty of the people, whose common sense is in the end the sole arbiter.

Misunderstandings and petty quarrels between individuals often occur in even the happiest families; but they are composed amicably, without resort to knife or pistol. So should it be in the case of bickering between nations. And in the same way that members of a family have equal rights, so it should be granted that nations have equality of status. No nation can be ostracized or held in a position of inferiority to its fellows. Any nation so treated will become an enemy, never a friend, of the international union; to which faith and trust are indispensable for its maintenance.

But the world is in peril because of the lack of that faith. Governments, distrusting treaty makers, no longer hold treaties in respect; regarding them as merely temporary make-shifts. Lasting agreement, permanent mutual understanding, have to be founded on truth and honesty. A pledged word ought to be as binding on the State as on the individual. In ordinary private life a partner to a contract is bound by law; the State should be bound by honor.

A distinguished scholar and profound thinker, the President of Columbia University, in words spoken not long ago, has emphasized the fact that the fundamental evil in our day is the world-wide lack of confidence.

He points out, too, that the nations of the world are now precisely where the thirteen American States were after they had gained independence and before they had organized a federal form of government.

In his opinion, world organization, world consultation, and cooperation are essential to world prosperity and international peace; as essential for the nations of the world today as for the thirteen independent, competitive, and self-centered States of America in the eighteenth century.

I believe he is right. To my mind, his are wise words. When mankind has matured in wisdom, it will be generally accepted that international interests are inseparably interwoven. So I ask you young men to inculcate, by example and precept, this principle. Steadfastly maintain your own national rights; but recognize the similar rights of other nations, as bound up with yours.

When that is universally appreciated, such epithets as militarist and pacifist will disappear; obsolete, forgotten; and none of us will be afraid to stand forth and say—with Abou ben Adhem—"Write me as one that loves his fellow men."

THE RESPONSIBILITY OF GOVERNMENTS AND PEOPLES[5]

By the Honorable Cordell Hull
Secretary of State of the United States

It is a great satisfaction to me to be able to welcome in the name of the Government of the United States the distinguished members of the Third World Power Conference and the Second Congress of the International Commission on Large Dams. I assure you that it affords us genuine pleasure to have you as our guests in the nation's capital.

The subject of the development and use of power, the harnessing of the forces of nature to make them work for man, is of tremendous and increasing importance. Your meeting here in Washington is convincing proof of that assertion.

Engineers in every specialized field, producers of fuel, operators of plants and distributors of power, and prominent government officials have come here from more than fifty nations for the purpose of meeting together to exchange technical knowledge, experiences, and opinions.

Opportunities for Service Cited

Power represents one of the largest single factors in any nation's economic structure; for upon power depend to a large extent industry, transportation, communications, and, to a growing degree, agriculture. And as the uses of power are extended to millions of people throughout the world, the influence upon society of this great expansion must have the careful consideration of us all.

Those of you who are concerned with the the development of power technology, and those of you who are interested in the organization and use of power resources, have before you almost unlimited opportunities for great service to mankind. Inventive and engineering genius have brought many of the luxuries of two decades ago within the reach of all today. Power and mechanical appliances conceived and produced by men of your training and experience are able to provide an even greater abundance of good things.

But they also are capable of producing machines of destruction—engines of war. Unfortunately, a vastly disproportionate share of the skill and energy of scientists and statesmen alike is being devoted

[5] Address delivered before the Third World Power Conference and the Second Congress of the International Commission on Large Dams, Washington, D. C., September 7, 1936.

now in many parts of the world to the creation and organization of forces of destruction.

Shall we allow this application of genius and energy to be dissipated in the agony of armed conflict, or shall we insist with all the determination at our command that they be employed objectively in the pursuits of peace? Shall the brains of the world be used to lighten the burdens of man, or shall they be used for the grim purposes of war?

The responsibility of maintaining peace in a world fraught with suspicion and fear, and torn by dangerous ambitions and conflicting political philosophies, rests not upon governments alone. This responsibility rests to even greater degree upon the shoulders of the thinking people of each land; people such as you who meet here to consider important matters common to every country.

You meet in a spirit of friendly cooperation with no thought of chauvinism or political jealousy. You thus not only make progress in your own field of endeavor; you also advance the cause of peace. And the cause of peace is the cause of civilization; religion, science, culture, and social betterment only go forward in a world without war.

Every war of the past has retarded the progress of civilization in direct proportion to the vigor with which it was pursued and the number of days, months, or years it has endured. Yet we find today a lamentable absence of appreciation by many responsible and influential statesmen that these present warlike tendencies can only lead to a world holocaust.

Urges Spreading of Lesson

Are we in this supposedly enlightened age so stupid that we cannot read this awful lesson of history? I refuse to believe that we are. I am convinced that once this lesson is fully learned by the people of the world the unanimity of their response will secure to us the blessings of permanent peace.

And it is your duty as well as mine to teach this lesson. The people of the world must learn that war is a cruel mill whose stones are the misled hope of national aggrandizement and the selfish ambitions of unscrupulous persons.

The oil and fuel of that mill are furnished by the fear and hate which come from distrust and suspicion. The grain for that mill is the valiant, patriotic youth of the world, ready to carry out the orders of the leaders, who are too often reckless or ruthless. The grist from that mill is death—death to youth, death to hope, death to civilization!

Accustomed as you are, as men of science or men of affairs, to deal with tangible things and with exact facts, you are essentially realists. I think the definition of realism as applied to international relations has greatly changed in the recent past.

From the end of the World War up to a short time ago, those who labored to bring about the settlement of differences among nations by peaceful means were termed impractical idealists. The realists were those who put no faith in those efforts for the peaceful settlement of international disputes. They refused to believe in the possible effectiveness of this work for peace, and held that it was futile to attempt to settle differences between nations except by the judgment of the sword.

"Fabric of Peace Worn Thin"

But today the true realist in international affairs knows that, in the face of present threats, our efforts to devise ways and means of preserving the peace must be redoubled. The true realist is he who knows that the fabric of peace has been worn perilously thin; that if it is again torn asunder by the bloody hands of war it may never be repaired.

I spoke a moment ago of the great responsibility of governments and peoples to preserve the peace. In all history the weight of that responsibility has never been so great as at this hour.

The world has countless times in the past known the horror and destruction of war. In each case it has labored back to the sanity of peace, sometimes quickly, sometimes only after long dark years of struggle. But the wars of the past, with the exception of the world conflict which began in 1914, give us no basis for judging the effects of a war of the future.

If war comes upon us, it will be fought not alone by uniformed armies and navies but by the entire populations of the countries involved. Airplanes, poison gas, and other modern fighting equipment of which we can only conjecture would make the world a veritable inferno.

A general war now would set loose forces that would be beyond control—forces which might easily bring about a virtual destruction of modern political thought, with all its achievements, and possibly a veritable shattering of our civilization.

Calls for Sane Perspective

Our one hope is that the governments and peoples of the world may fully realize the solemn responsibility which rests upon them all and that realistic envisaging of the inevitable consequences will prevent their flying at each other's throats no matter how great may be their impulses and the fancied incentives.

There exists today an unparalleled opportunity for those nations and groups which look forward with clear vision to bring about an early return to sane perspectives and relationships based upon full comprehension that the members of the family of nations must live together amicably and work together in peace or be broken in an utterly destructive misuse of the power and the instruments which, properly used, bear beneficial witness to the amazing constructive capacity of mankind.

I cannot too strongly urge that, with the great capacity which you possess and the influence which you can wield, you, the members of this congress, and your associates in every land, bend your efforts unceasingly toward perfecting programs of methods for the preservation and promotion of peace. I urge that you insist that the products of your constructive thought and efforts be devoted to constructive ends.

491

EUROPE AT THE CROSSROADS[6]

By Kamil Krofta
Minister of Foreign Affairs of Czechoslovakia

In the speech which I had the honor of making some time ago in the Foreign Affairs Committees of the Chamber of Deputies and Senate, I discussed the situation which had arisen through the denunciation of the Locarno Treaty by Germany on the 7th of March last, and I formulated the Czechoslovak standpoint towards that grave event.

On that occasion I confined myself to a juridical and political analysis of the questions connected with a breach of the Locarno agreements, then in the forefront of public interest everywhere, and left it to a later opportunity to deal with the situation as a whole, and to outline our standpoint to the events taking place abroad and to the questions which concern Czechoslovakia.

When Dr. Beneš, the then Minister of Foreign Affairs and now President of the Republic, opened his speech on foreign affairs on the 5th of November, 1935, he characterized the situation as follows:

> After several years of labor on the part of the Disarmament Conference, we have to confess that it has so far been found impossible to arrive at agreement in regard to armaments, and that the individual States are once again compelled to devote vast effort and great financial outlay first and foremost to the organization of their armies. After difficult negotiations undertaken with the object of gaining fresh guarantees of security and peace on the basis of the pacts of security already concluded in Europe, we can only record partial success in this work, while on the other hand we find ourselves quite unexpectedly in the midst of a war which is raging, it is true, on the African Continent, but which also casts its grave shadows upon the continent of Europe. This conflict has resulted, too, in serious differences between the European Great Powers and has culminated for the first time in the sixteen years' existence of the League of Nations in collective action by almost all the members of the Geneva institution against another member, against Italy, designated by the Council of the League as the aggressor, and thus falling under the sanctions laid down in Article 16 of the League Covenant.

Today, when we examine the situation as it has now developed following the unsuccessful effort made by Sir Samuel Hoare and

[6] Speech delivered before the Foreign Affairs Committee of both Houses of the National Assembly, May 28, 1936. Reprinted by permission from *Czechoslovak Sources and Documents*, No. 10, 1936.

M. Laval to bring about peace in Abyssinia, following the occupation of the Rhineland by Germany, the victory of the Italian expedition in Abyssinia, and the promulgation of an Italian Empire of Abyssinia, it is impossible to hide the fact that the events which have occurred since the last speech made by Dr. Beneš as Foreign Minister have not improved the international situation, but on the contrary have introduced new and grave elements of disquiet into the life of the nations of Europe. In the course of those six months we have seen that a State, for whose security a great majority of the members of the League of Nations gave their voices, has been compelled to abandon its resistance, we have seen that a unilateral breach of international obligations has not been made good, and we have seen in this last fact what a dangerous rôle in international politics can be played by the element of surprise.

All these happenings, combined with the economic crisis that has for a number of years weighed so heavily upon Europe, veil the political horizon and the prospects for the future in dark gloom. It would, of course, be wrong to see only the dark sides of the prevailing situation, and to shut our eyes to several bright points which are to be perceived. We must not, however, be blind to the fact that the present international situation, though perhaps it does not arouse fears of immediate serious conflict, lays upon us the duty of the utmost vigilance.

The Italo-Abyssinian Conflict

The war between Italy and Abyssinia which broke out last autumn and called forth, as is well known, sanctions on the part of the League of Nations against Italy, came to an end this spring as far as operations in the field are concerned. After several decisive military successes, the Italian army scattered the remnants of the defeated Abyssinian troops and entered Addis Ababa, the capital, which the Emperor of Abyssinia had already abandoned. The Supreme Fascist Council and the Italian Cabinet Council proclaimed on May 9th the annexation of Abyssinia, and the King of Italy assumed for himself and his successors the title of Emperor of Abyssinia.

Thus the warlike conflict between Italy and Abyssinia, after holding the world in suspense for more than six months, ended with the defeat of Abyssinia, and will now, when the Italians are no longer faced with any organized armies, have considerable effect upon the future development of foreign policy.

At the beginning of last year, as is well known, M. Laval, the French Premier, and Signor Mussolini signed at Rome a protocol which settled questions at issue between Italy and France, and included an agreement on Central European policy. At Stresa on the 11th to 14th April, 1935, a further agreement was arrived at between those Powers and England, in which England, France, and Italy took a joint stand against the armament of Germany and expressed themselves in favor of the negotiation of an Eastern and a Danubian Pact. A breach was made in this so-called "Stresa Front" by the Italo-Abyssinian conflict, in which, as is well known, both England and France opposed the aggressor. The attempt made by Sir Samuel Hoare and M. Laval to contribute to a settlement of the conflict by peace proposals in December, 1935, failed, both the parties at war rejecting these proposals. This involved a failure of the attempt to restore the Stresa Front, that is, agreement between England, France, and Italy. Although France was inclined, even after these failures, to assist in settling the dispute, no further attempts at conciliation were made, particularly since France was fully occupied with the matter of Germany's entry into the Rhine zone. Thus the end of the Abyssinian war finds the Powers most concerned in different positions, and for the present it cannot be said that these Great Powers have made any substantial approach towards one another. Such, at any rate, was the impression given by the last meeting of the Council of the League of Nations which was held on the 12th May, that is, since the annexation of Abyssinia, for the Council merely decided unanimously to reassemble on the 15th June and to make no change for the present in the measure jointly adopted by the member States of the League. In other words, they decided to uphold the sanctions.

The decision for common action by the members of the League of Nations against Italy was taken by the Council of the League on 7th October, 1935, when the Council declared that the Italian Government by commencing warlike operations against Abyssinia, a member of the League, had violated Article 12 of the Covenant of the League, according to which no member of the League may begin a war with another member as long as the consideration of the dispute commenced before the Council has not been completed. From that moment, then, all the members of the League of Nations had the right and the duty to apply sanctions according to Article 16 against Italy, for the Covenant provides that a unanimous decision on the part of the State members of the Council that some State has violated the Covenant *ipso facto* signifies the application of the sanctions without any further resolutions.

By the decision of the Assembly of the League of Nations of the 9th-11th October, 1935, fifty members of the Assembly adopted the same standpoint as the Council, and accepted a recommendation that the members of the Assembly should appoint a co-ordinating committee for the application of the sanctions under Article 16 of the Covenant. This committee at once took up its functions, and adopted the first measures for carrying out the sanctions. According to the report of the committee of experts of the League of Nations, submitted to the League at the beginning of February last, fifty-two States participated in the prohibition of the import of arms to Italy, fifty-two took part in the financial sanctions, fifty in the prohibition of the import of merchandise to Italy, while fifty-one States adopted the prohibition of the export of certain goods to Italy.

Czechloslovakia's attitude to the Italo-Abyssinian conflict was formulated as early as the 5th November, 1935, by Dr. Beneš, the then Minister of Foreign Affairs, in the following terms: "Czechoslovakia is neutral in this question and will remain so; she does not interfere in the actual dispute between Italy and Abyssinia, nor will interfere in the future. In so far as she is compelled directly or indirectly to deal with the dispute in any way, she does so solely and exclusively on the basis of decisions made at Geneva by the League of Nations and binding on all members of the League."

Czechoslovakia has remained faithful to this standpoint throughout the whole conflict. We have fulfilled, and continue to fulfil, the obligations which arise for us out of our membership of the League of Nations, striving at the same time to maintain not only an absolutely correct but also a friendly attitude towards Italy. As a State which does not desire to, and indeed cannot, surrender the advantages accruing to it from the League of Nations, we could not of course allow our actions to deny the principles of collective security and assistance, the application of which we might one day be called upon to ask for ourselves. Being members of the League of Nations we could not act otherwise than according to the duty laid upon us by the Covenant. We cannot direct our course by a double type of morality—one system for ourselves and a second one for others. The League of Nations although it was unable to fulfil all its tasks as we should have wished and according to the valid decisions made at Geneva, is a political reality with which the Great Powers reckon for the protection of their interests and with which we too must reckon. If we have no more perfect international institution for the present than is the League of Nations, we have at least it.

I hope that our standpoint will be everywhere understood. From the very outset of the Italo-Abyssinian conflict we sincerely desired to see the obstacles to an understanding removed by agreement among the Great Powers. In the present situation we desire nothing more than to see England and France speedily arrive at an understanding with Italy, with due regard, of course, also to the interests and the fate of the League of Nations and we hope that such understanding will result in the speedy restoration of normal conditions. In the meantime we await the final decision of Geneva and shall loyally act according to it.

Negotiations with Germany

In the speech which I made on the 17th March last I described the events leading up to the military occupation of the demilitarized zone by Germany, what were the first reactions to this obvious breach of the Peace Treaty, and what standpoint we took to that unfortunate event. Today I will attempt to outline in brief the further development of events.

The Council of the League of Nations, to which the matter had been referred by the French and Belgian Governments, passed on the 19th March last, in the presence of German delegates who had been invited to the deliberations, the following resolution:

> The Council of the League of Nations declares, in response to the application made by Belgium and France on the 8th March, 1936, that the German Government has violated Article 43 of the Treaty of Versailles by allowing military detachments to occupy the zone demilitarized under Article 42 et seq. of the Peace Treaty and the Locarno agreements. The Council requests the secretary-general to inform the signatory Powers without delay of this its resolution.

The English, Belgian, French, and Italian Governments by mutual agreement on the basis of this resolution then handed a comprehensive memorandum to the German Government. It is essential to deal in somewhat more detail with that memorandum, for it is an important basis for further negotiation.

In the introductory paragraphs of the memorandum the Powers state that a conscientious observance and fulfilment of treaties is a fundamental principle of international life and a condition for the preservation of peace that, according to the existing principles of international law, no State has the right, without the consent of the contracting parties, to release itself from the obligations of a treaty or to alter its terms, and the action of Germany in violating the Treaty of Versailles and the Treaty of Locarno is in conflict with those principles. In subsequent paragraphs the Powers state that they regard the provisions of the Locarno Treaty as still valid, and that they have empowered the general staffs of their armies to enter into touch with one another and make technical preparations for defense against unprovoked attack. The Great Powers recommend Germany to submit her objections to the validity of the Locarno agreements to the Permanent Court of International Justice at The Hague.

For the intervening period before agreement between Germany and the Powers should be arrived at, the memorandum demanded the following provisional measures on the part of Germany:

1. All movement of troops and material into the demilitarized zone to be stopped.

2. No military formations in that area to be increased beyond the footing of the 7th March, 1936.

3. No fortifications or aerodromes to be established in the demilitarized zone.

The French and Belgian Governments in their turn undertook that during the period in question they would cease the dispatch of troops to the frontiers. The Powers further stated that they were considering the dispatch of an international armed corps into a zone which would extend twenty kilometers to the east of the Belgian and French frontiers, and the establishment of an international commission to superintend the observance of the military conditions imposed upon Germany.

If the German Government, continued the memorandum, accepted the conditions of the Great Powers, Germany would be able to take part in a conference, the program of which would include the proposals made by the German Chancellor on the 7th March, 1936, a change in the Rhine Statute and the agreement for mutual aid concluded among the Locarno Powers, open to all the signatories of Locarno, and designed to increase that security.

As regards Belgium, France, Great Britain, and Italy, the designed increase in security was, according to the memorandum to be attained in particular by a provision for mutual aid, by a guaranty of speedy action on the part of the signatories in case of need, and by technical preparations for such measures as would ensure a carrying out of the obligations undertaken.

In a further section of the memorandum the Great Powers outlined the program of a coming great international conference, the agenda of which would include:

1. an agreement concerning a precise and effective system of collective security with special reference to the question of how to apply the provisions of Article 16 of the Covenant of the League of Nations,

2. disarmament,

3. improvement of economic relations between the different countries,

4. the question of agreement concerning non-aggression between Germany, Austria, and Czechoslovakia, and the question of the entry of Germany into the League of Nations, and a possible revision of the Covenant of the League.

The memorandum is plainly a work of compromise, and its great importance lies in the fact that England, Belgium, France, and Italy publicly manifested their unity in the questions which arose through the occupation of the Rhineland by Germany. By publicly proclaiming the Treaty of Locarno as still valid, by announcing a collaboration of their general staffs in the event of an unprovoked attack, and by expressing themselves in favor of preserving the existing system of security until a new one can be elaborated, they contributed in no small measure to a pacification of perturbed public opinion. Moreover the memorandum signifies, of course, that the Great Powers were willing, on certain conditions, to negotiate with Germany for a new adjustment of security on the basis of the German proposals.

The demands of the Western Powers that Germany should submit the dispute to the decision of the International Court at The Hague, that she should not fortify the occupied zone, and that she should consent to the dispatch of international troops to the German frontier zone, were, according to the interpretation given them by Mr. Anthony Eden, the British Secretary of State for Foreign Affairs, in the House of Commons on the 26th of March last, only meant as proposals and not as an ultimatum or dictate, so that the German Government could put forward their counter proposals.

Discussing the pact of non-aggression in the West Mr. Eden said:

> The scheme is that there should be, as suggested by the German Chancellor, a number of non-aggression pacts; that in Western Europe these non-aggression pacts should be guaranteed by Britain and Italy. That is the German Chancellor's scheme; but over and above that, in our own proposals there will be pacts of mutual assistance between the Powers of Western Europe which would differ from Locarno in this: that the guarantees would be reciprocal, and that we should share with others in the guarantees as well as in the risks. Those mutual assistance pacts would, of course, be open to all the signatories of Locarno including Germany.

This interpretation by the British Foreign Secretary of the German proposal of a new Locarno gives that proposal unusual importance. It obviously means that England was ready in case of a European conflict to undertake under certain conditions to render help, and that she would claim analogous help for herself from the European Powers on the basis of agreements. This would be a substantial departure from the Locarno Treaty. Whereas in that Treaty England was merely one of the guarantors with Italy of the French and Belgian frontiers, she would now be ready to guarantee not merely the Belgian and French frontiers but also those of Italy and Germany on condition that those Powers mutually undertook to guarantee each others' frontiers and the frontiers of England.

In addition to the points of general importance, we are interested in the fact that the program of international conferences includes also the question of pacts of non-aggression between Czechoslovakia and Germany. To this it may be added that it will be the endeavor of Czechoslovakia, in case of negotiations with Germany for insuring the frontiers of her neighbors, to conduct these negotiations on a European basis, that is, in combination with negotiations for insuring the frontiers of Germany's western neighbors. It may be recalled that a similar endeavor was made during the negotiations for the Locarno Treaty.

This effort on the part of Czechoslovakia is based, on the one hand, on the conviction that peace in Europe is indivisible, that is, that a threat to the frontiers of any European State whatsoever is a grave menace to peace throughout Europe, and on the other hand, on the fact that Czechoslovakia like Poland is already a partner in a system of security in the west by virtue of her guaranty treaty with France concluded at Locarno on the 16th October, 1925.

The attitude taken by Germany to the plan of the Locarno Powers is well known: Germany rejected the conditions laid down in the memorandum according to which further negotiations were to be opened, on the ground that such negotiations would mean a continuation of the old acts of discrimination intolerable to a great nation, and represent an attempt to subject Germany to a new unequal treatment as compared with other countries. Germany further expressed the opinion that a genuine and lasting peace can only be based on the free will of nations enjoying equal rights, and she expressed her readiness to submit new proposals to be sent to the British Government.

The promised answer was handed to the British Government on the 1st of April last. In the first part of the document Germany appeals to her right to equality of status with the other nations, explains from her standpoint why she was justified in occupying the Rhineland with her military forces, rejects the suggestion of submitting the dispute to the International Court, protests against the proposed collaboration of the general staffs, and develops a peace plan of her own. That peace plan, according to the German proposal, would be carried out in three stages. The first period, lasting about four months, would be devoted to gradually calming the atmosphere, and elucidating the procedure for the negotiations to be initiated. The Germans would be prepared to give the assurance that they would not undertake any reinforcement of their troops in the Rhineland during that period, and would not move their troops closer to the Belgian and French frontiers, provided the Belgian and French Governments acted similarly. The carrying out of these guarantees of security would be entrusted to a frontier commission, composed of representatives of the western Powers and representatives of neutral States. The second period would be devoted to actual negotiations for the conclusion of a pact of non-aggression or security between France and Belgium on the one part and Germany on the other for a term of twenty-five years. Germany would agree to this pact being guaranteed by England and Italy and she is ready to accept the obligation of military aid which would accrue from the conclusion of the pact.

Czechoslovakia is directly touched by section 17 of the German memorandum by which the declaration made by the German Chancellor on 7th March last, in which he spoke of a pact of non-aggression with Germany's Eastern neighbors, is supplemented to the extent that Germany expresses her willingness to enter into negotiations for pacts of non-aggression with the States on her southeastern and northeastern frontiers, thus removing the misunderstanding as if Germany had taken up a different attitude in the question of the security of Czechoslovakia and Austria from that which she had adopted in regard to the security of her other neighbors on the east.

Comparing the German answer with the proposals made in the memorandum presented by England, Belgium, France, and Italy, we see that Germany declines to accept the conditions as formulated in the memorandum, but that, on the other hand, her suggestions concerning the organization of security on the east and west make some approach to the basis on which the Great Powers signified their willingness to enter upon further negotiations.

The German reply was received, as was to be expected, with reserve, for it failed to satisfy in several points. The French objections have been formulated in a lengthy note sent on the 8th April to the Governments of Belgium, Britain, and Italy, and the note was accompanied by a peace plan and the French view concerning a rehabilitation of economic conditions. This is a comprehensive document, elaborated with profound knowledge of the matter, and containing many very notable suggestions. The note deals in detail with the German reply to accusations of a violation of rights, reproaches Germany with not desiring in any way to meet the demands of the other Locarno Powers, defines the view of the French Government on the question of collective security and mutual assistance, and demands a security that is supported by guarantees for the countries bordering on Germany and for Russia.

The French note, although on the whole it regards the German answer to the memorandum as unsatisfactory, does not represent a definitive rejection of the German proposals. The series of questions put in the note as well as the circumstance that France has put orward a plan of her own against the German one, bear witness to the fact that the French Government is willing to enter upon further negotiations. An expression of this tendency—which has moreover been emphasized by England ever since the beginning of the conflict —was seen in the resolution passed by the Locarno Powers on 10th April last, when England, Belgium, France, and Italy declared that the German reply made no contribution to a renewal of the confidence essential for the immediate commencement of negotiations, but that it would be advisable to elucidate several points in the German reply, especially those dealt with in the French note. The Powers further agreed that the general staff discussions, which they reported to Germany in their memorandum, should commence on the 15th April. These general staff talks have actually taken place as between the English, French, and Belgian staffs, but no representatives of the Italian general staff were present. The questions which it was announced the British Government had to ask were also submitted to the German Government through the British Ambassador in Berlin. These questions refer to all points on which the previous proposals of the two parties substantially differed. So far the German answer to these questions has not yet been received.

As will be seen, the Great Powers have not got very far in the discussion of the dispute with Germany. Since the occupation of the Rhineland by German troops more than two and half months have elapsed, and negotiations have proceeded no further than to a preliminary exchange of views. It would be great optimism to contend that this is a splendid result, but in the sphere of foreign politics patience is more essential than perhaps anywhere else.

Notwithstanding the meager outcome, the negotiations so far have produced one or two positive facts which deserve emphasis. In the first place all the decisions made have been arrived at by agreement among the interested Powers, and in particular agreement between England and France has been preserved and publicly manifested. Secondly the necessity has been universally recognized of replacing the system of Locarno agreements by a new system of security and of solving at the same time in that connection the question of the security of Czechoslovakia and Austria. Finally Germany herself has expressed her willingness to enter the League of Nations, and says that is is part of her plan to solve not only the political questions that remain open but also the questions centering round the economic recovery of Europe.

Should an agreement be arrived at in the near future between the League and Italy, it is possible to hope that negotiations with Germany will progress more rapidly and successfully.

Central Europe: The Hodža Plan, the Rome Pact, the Little Entente

Up to the year 1929 the whole world enjoyed economic prosperity. Even the Central European States, although for the most part only recently established on their own territories and only then beginning to function as independent units, gave during this period of prosperity proofs that their political and economic existence was fully justified. It is only natural that the economic crisis which so profoundly affected countries whose territories had for centuries represented well-proven economic entities should have still more seriously shaken the economic organism of new States. When we see how even the big and economically powerful States, at the first onset of a currency devaluation crisis, introduced a system of exchange restrictions, strove to remedy the unfavorable character of their trade balance by limiting imports and by preventing the free outflow of exchange, how they suffered, and still suffer, through inability to find work for their millions of unemployed, we cannot wonder that all these things caused even greater losses to the smaller States, especially those which had not had time to accumulate reserves enough to sustain them through the period of emergency.

Since one of the external signs of the crisis, at least in the early stages, was an unusual decline in agricultural prices, countries in which agricultural output is one of the main economic factors naturally suffered twofold. It stands to reason that measures which such countries were compelled to take to alleviate the crisis had to be more radical than those adopted elsewhere, but that this again hindered the normal interchange of goods with other countries dependent upon that interchange.

The economic crisis gave a considerable impulse to the idea that much could be gained by economic cooperation in Central Europe, and that one of the causes of the aggravated severity of the crisis in that part of the Continent could be eliminated. Czechoslovakia has always been in favor of such cooperation, but she desired a purely economic cooperation, free of all specific political influences from whatever quarter they might come; she wished Yugoslavia and Rumania to be partners, and she desired first to secure the approval of the Western European Great Powers, that is, not only of France and Great Britain, but also of Germany and Italy.

I will make only a brief reference to the more important schemes put forward:

1. The plan of the French Government of 1931 proposed the establishment of a Central Sales Bureau for Central European grain, with special advantages for Austria, an international agreement among the industries, and loans for the Central European States.

2. The Tardieu plan of 1932 included a proposal for preference among the Central European States for both agricultural and industrial output. This plan failed because only the small States of Central Europe and not the Great Powers were to participate in the preferences.

3. Following the failure of the Tardieu plan, the Lausanne Conference in July, 1932, appointed a Committee entrusted with the task of elaborating for the European Commission of Study proposals for the economic rehabilitation of Central and Eastern Europe. The committee met at Stresa early in September, 1932, and drew up a series of recommendations. Among other things they recommended the conclusion of an agreement for the disposal of Central and Eastern European grain. The proposal for this agreement was based on the idea that the Central European States should, by means of bilateral treaties, either grant preferences in favor of this grain, or should contribute to the so-called "Revalorization Fund" which was to be established.

The European Commission of Study in October, 1932, accepted the recommendations of the Stresa Conference, but they were not put into effect. Only two treaties granting preferences to Austria were concluded. These were the Franco-Austrian commercial agreement of 29th December, 1932, under which France granted preferences in favor of Austrian timber, and the Polish Austrian agreement of 11th November, 1933, under which Poland granted preferences in favor of a number of Austrian industrial products.

4. The Italian plan of 1933 recommended for Central Europe a preferential system by means of bilateral agreements not only for certain categories of agricultural products but also for industrial output with, however, certain limitations which proved the death of the plan.

The failure of these schemes, which had the support of the Great Powers, shows how difficult it is to solve the problem of economic cooperation in Central Europe. The difficulties lie in the circumstance that the questions to be solved are complicated not only from the economic but also from the political angle, that is to say, for the reason that the economic problem of Central Europe has also an important political aspect.

The Czechoslovak Government is well aware of this fact, and therefore collaborates with the Yugoslav and Rumanian Governments with the object of making the Little Entente alliance, originally a political alliance, into an economic alliance too. By the establishment of an Economic Council of the Little Entente, and the elaboration of a plan for the economic rapprochement of the States of the Little Entente—a plan which is now being systematically carried out—a basis was formed which can prove the starting point for their collaboration in the economic sphere with the other Central European States.

It was on this basis that the Czechoslovak Prime Minister, Dr. Hodža, in his then function of Minister of Foreign Affairs, began early this year a series of consultations on economic collaboration in Central Europe. The Prime Minister has himself formulated on more than one occasion his views of Central Europe in this connection, and I shall therefore confine myself to the main outlines of his observations.

Visible elements of Central European economic consolidation, says Dr. Hodža, already exist in the form of cooperation between several groups of States, as illustrated by the efforts made by the Baltic States, the Little Entente, the States of the Rome bloc, and those of the Balkan bloc. It is essential first of all to devote attention to economic rapprochement between the States of the Little Entente and those of the Rome Pact, that is, the Danubian States. It is advisable to proceed from the partial to the general in this case, for the reason that the fate of Central European economic consolidation rests upon agreement between Czechoslovakia, Yugoslavia, and Rumania on the one side, and Hungary and Austria on the other.

These States should agree upon the following minimum program:

1. not to increase the existing customs duties, and not to levy duties on goods that have hitherto been exempt from duty,

2. to maintain the *status quo*, that is, not to worsen the conditions

for mutual exchange of merchandise, and to preserve the preferences already granted.

Hodža's ideas found an echo in the lecture given by Dr. Kurt von Schuschnigg, the Austrian Chancellor, on the occasion of his visit to Prague on the 16th of January last. Discussing plans for economic cooperation in Central Europe, the Austrian Chancellor said:

Attempts at a regional solution in the sphere of commercial policy are to be seen not only in the agreement of the States of the Little Entente for the establishment of their Economic Council, but also in the Rome tripartite agreements which may well become a factor of the regeneration of Central European economy. The building up of close economic collaboration among the neighboring Danubian States is an essential primary condition of economic rehabilitation. This goal can best be reached in stages by the path of economic association and understanding among these countries to the absolute exclusion of the political side. It has been shown that the granting of mutual preferences is possible, is effective, and useful.

Dr. Hodža availed himself of the Austrian Chancellor's visit to Prague to discuss with him several questions of interest to both countries, particularly questions of an economic nature. Both agreed that it was in the interests of the two States that the negotiations for a commercial treaty between Czechoslovakia and Austria should be concluded as speedily as possible, that the treaty of conciliation and arbitration signed some years ago should be prolonged and steps taken to extend its provisions.

At the beginning of February last the Prime Minister paid a visit to Paris where he was in touch with the leading personalities concerned with French foreign policy, and informed them of his views on the questions of the consolidation of conditions in Central Europe. In Paris the Premier also met M. Titulescu, the Rumanian Minister of Foreign Affairs, and the chairman of the Balkan Entente, M. Rudshi Aras, the Turkish Foreign Minister.

On the 22nd-24th of February Dr. Hodža paid a visit to Belgrade and conferred with Dr. Stoyadinović, the Yugoslav Premier. The two Premiers, with the approval of the Rumanian Foreign Minister, agreed that experts representing the governments of their three countries should, on the occasion of the conference of the Economic Council of the Little Entente at Prague, discuss the concrete proposals put forward by Dr. Hodža, and this was done on the 7th-8th of March last. The consultations of the experts will be continued in due course.

During the visit of the Austrian Chancellor, Dr. von Schuschnigg, to Prague, the Czechoslovak Premier, as already noted, conferred with him concerning the commercial treaty for which negotiations had for some considerable time been proceeding in Vienna. Early in March the Prime Minister visited Vienna to return the visit paid by the Chancellor to Prague, and on this occasion the two statesmen signed on the 10th March a protocol in which it was stated that they had examined the progress made in the negotiations, had come to agreement on outstanding points, and decided that the treaty should include preferences according to the recommendations made by the Stresa Conference.

The commercial treaty between Czechoslovakia and Austria which was signed on the 2nd April, 1936, is an important and extensive document which has taken the place of the already obsolete treaty of the year 1921. The treaty, which settles all the open questions of economic contact between the two countries, includes on the part of Austria preferential treatment for a number of Czechoslovak agricultural products, while Czechoslovakia in return grants preferences for certain Austrian industrial output.

The negotiations themselves, and then the signature of the treaty, attracted great attention on the part of public opinion both here and abroad. The German Government has even made a protest against the preferences which Czechoslovakia and Austria have granted one another reciprocally, on the ground that they were granted without agreement with Germany. The Czechoslovak Government, recognizing the interest which all countries, with whom Czechoslovakia has concluded commercial treaties based on most-favored-nation treatment, have in the Czechoslovak-Austrian treaty, informed them of the contents of that treaty and asked for their consent to the preferences. This request was also made to the German Government, but a reply has not yet been received.

The Rome Protocols

Shortly after the occupation of the Rhineland by Germany an event occurred of importance for Central Europe: the conclusion of the supplementary protocols to the Rome protocols of the year 1934.

Three such supplementary protocols were signed on 23rd March last by Signor Mussolini, the Italian Premier, Dr. von Schuschnigg, the Austrian Chancellor, and M. Gömbös, the Hungarian Premier. In the first of them the Premiers express their satisfaction at the favorable results produced by the continued collaboration of their three governments in the cause of preservation of peace and of the economic adjustment of Europe, they confirm their determination to abide faithfully by the undertakings binding Italy, Austria, and Hungary, and they decide to constitute themselves into a group and to establish for this purpose a standing organ for mutual consultation.

In the second supplementary protocol the representatives of the three States respectively confirm their resolution not to undertake any important political action concerning the Danubian question with the government of any third State without previously consulting the other two governments that signed the Rome protocols of 17th March, 1934. Although all the three governments are completely unanimous in their view of the value of an expansion of economic contacts with the other Danubian States, they realize that an intensification of those contacts is possible only by means of bilateral agreements.

The third supplementary protocol contains the resolution that the standing organ for mutual consultation shall be composed of the Foreign Ministers of the three signatory States. This organ will meet periodically, and at times when all the three governments regard a meeting as advisable.

The countries of the so-called "Rome bloc" have, it will be seen, laid down in these supplementary protocols hard and fast rules for the mutual contacts the foundations of which were laid by the Rome protocols as early as March, 1934.

It is of interest to us that what has happened in this case is similar to the action of the Little Entente in constituting its Statute of Organization. One of the very important provisions of the protocols in that the three States have founded their standing organ for mutual consultation, and that the meetings of this new organ are to be obligatory within certain but not actually defined periods. Not less important is the provision that none of the States of this group may enter upon important political negotiations with the government of a third State without previous agreement with the other two governments. For negotiations of an economic character the provisions are not so strict, for bilateral agreements are recommended, approval thus being indirectly expressed of the Czechoslovak-Austrian commercial treaty.

The Rome supplementary protocols do not lay down any new directives for the policy of the States of the Rome group. We must therefore assume that the fundamental trend of the foreign policy of Italy, Hungary, and Austria has undergone no change, and that the supplementary protocols are an expression of a determination to continue that line of policy. As a member of the Little Entente, the aim of which is political and economic collaboration among all members, Czechoslovakia welcomes concentric efforts in Central Europe, efforts which are directed towards the same goal as those of the Little Entente. Czechoslovakia does not therefore look with disfavor upon the fact that the States of the Rome group have drawn closer together, though she does not shut her eyes to the fact that the Rome group differs from the Little Entente in having a great Power within its ranks.

The Little Entente

The meeting of the Standing Council of the Little Entente was held on the 6th and 7th of May last in circumstances of special gravity from the political point of view. From many sides voices were heard—in some cases prompted by good will, in others, however, by the desire to cause confusion in a situation already full of tension—raising doubts whether the Little Entente possessed enough inner force to enable her as an entity to meet all the problems of the present situation and to maintain the unity she has hitherto manifested. The answer which the Little Entente gave European public opinion must satisfy all who have recognized in the Little Entente throughout her existence a bulwark of peace and democracy in Central Europe, and may be taken as a warning by those who have looked forward to exploiting for their own ends any dissolution of the Little Entente. Once again, and more emphatically than ever before, the Little Entente has demonstrated that she wishes, as she has wished for the sixteen years of her existence, to uphold within the scope of the League of Nations the peace of the world and respect for international obligations, to collaborate in the work of peace, and to stand on guard against all attempts at upheaval in Central

Europe. The Little Entente desires now, as in the past, to cooperate with the western Powers in preserving the independence of Austria, and is determined to make a firm stand equally against revisionism as against the restoration of a dynasty, the presence of which in Central Europe would provoke most grave conflict in the Danubian basin.

The Little Entente has further declared that she will persevere with inflexible firmness in her efforts to preserve the peace of Europe. United by common aims, conscious of their duties, the Little Entente States are indissolubly bound one to the other. The policy of the Little Entente is profoundly and completely one, whether it be a matter of the relation of the three States to the League of Nations, their attitude to the question of Austria's independence, to a return of the Habsburg dynasty, to the question of treaty revision, or whether it is a matter of their relations to France or England, to Italy, Germany, Hungary, Bulgaria, Austria or Poland, to the Balkan States or to Soviet Russia. The three Little Entente States will thus act in absolute unity in their attitude to any of these countries.

In expressing a desire that the preparatory work of the Locarno Powers should be quickly concluded, the Little Entente emphasized the fact that she has a vital interest in the preservation of the Treaties of St. Germain, Trianon, and Neuilly, and will do everything in her power to see that her rights and interests are respected. The States of the Little Entente will never give their approval to the legalization of any act altering international agreements of which they are among the signatories, unless such alteration is discussed with them and agreed upon according to the principles of international law.

The Little Entente intends to persevere in efforts towards the rapprochement of the Danubian States, and once again proclaims her approval of the principle of economic cooperation with the Rome bloc and Germany.

The Foreign Ministers of the Little Entente, after thus emphasizing the principles of their joint foreign policy, discussed the individual concrete questions, and on all points arrived at complete agreement as regards their unity of action.

Demonstrating thus her complete unity, the Little Entente once again declared in clear and decisive terms her determination to persevere in joint creative effort with her allies and with all countries prompted by good will.

Czechoslovakia's Relations With Other Countries

In the concluding portion of my speech I will briefly mention Czechoslovakia's relations with one or two other countries. It is unnecessary to say that we continue to be bound to France not only by the traditional ties of long friendship but also by the bonds of practical interests, strengthened as they are not only by political treaties but also by the convictions that it is one of the foremost tasks of our State to labor with all its strength in the defense of right and justice and for the preservation of peace. Our treaty with Soviet Russia links up with the treaty between Russia and France, and falling as it does within the scope of the League of Nations represents, in our opinion, another important factor of peace in Europe. The joint endeavors of these three countries threaten no one, for they have expressly and exclusively the character of a defense against unprovoked attack.

Their friendly collaboration is to be regarded as constructive activity, the sole aim of which is to insure peace and to strengthen the idea underlying the League of Nations. Anyone who asserts that Czechoslovakia with her allies is designing an attack against any party whatsoever is either deceiving himself or is attempting to deceive others.

An official refutation has likewise been forthcoming of all the fabricated reports spread with obvious design concerning the alleged presence of Soviet troops in Slovakia and the construction of hangars for the Soviet air fleet, and so on. The States interested have received from us unequivocal and official information on these points. Mention is made of the matter in this place mainly too for the purpose of informing international public opinion of the origin of these unsupported rumors and of the object with which such reports are being spread. It is of course only natural that our relations with the Soviet Union have, since the conclusion of the Treaty of 1934, steadily grown in friendly character.

It was once said by Dr. Beneš that Czechoslovakia has no direct conflicts with Germany, and that she can only come into conflict with Germany as a reflex of all European disputes, for the European States are so mutually dependent on one another that general European peace is really indivisible. I am glad today to be able to state that as far as direct contacts between Czechoslovakia and the German Reich are concerned our mutual relations continue to be good.

In discussing the occupation of the Rhine zone I could not of course be silent on the subject of the dark shadows which that unsettled question is throwing on the international situation as a whole. We are not direct participants in that dispute, but we may perhaps be allowed to express the hope that a solution acceptable to all countries may be found which will disperse the tension that so gravely affects Europe now.

Relations with our eastern neighbor, Poland, have of late improved slightly. I am glad to be able to appreciate the fact that the wireless propaganda at Katovice directed against Czechoslovakia has ceased, and that the conditions at the Polish Consulate at Moravská Ostrava have taken a turn for the better. On the other hand expulsions of Czechoslovak subjects from Poland still continue, and they include cases where the victims have been settled for long years in Poland, and for whom a violent severance from the environment in which they have lived for years and become identified represents great moral distress and irreparable material damage. When it is answered on the Polish side that Czechoslovakia similarly expels Polish subjects, it is not out of place to remember that we waited long to see if the Polish authorities would cease to expel Czechoslovak subjects. When they did not cease, we had no alternative but to have recourse to a similar procedure, if only to be able to provide employment for our subjects banished from Poland.

Dr. Beneš, while still Minister of Foreign Affairs, in his speech to Parliament on the 5th November, 1935, said that our sincere willingness to submit all questions in dispute to an appropriate international forum continued. Two days later the Polish Press Bureau issued a communiqué in which the idea of arbitration was rejected on the Polish side. Arbitration, it was said, cannot be applied to a problem which is clearly and in binding form defined in the Czechoslovak Polish treaty of 23rd April, 1925. In view of the fact—so ran the communiqué—that on the Czechoslovak side the obligations undertaken in that treaty have not been fulfilled, the proposal of arbitration cannot but arouse the impression that the matter is to be protracted while oppression of the Polish population in Czech-Silesia is to continue. Dr. Beneš's declaration thus introduced no positive element into the mutual relations and was unsuccessful in removing the difficulties then existing. An improvement in these relations, it was stated at the close of the Polish communiqué, can only be achieved by a change in the attitude of the Czechoslovak Government to the Polish population, and not by any tactical gestures the aim of which is to arouse in the minds of the foreign public, and also in the minds of the Czechoslovak public who are uninformed as to the real state of affairs, the appearance of good will.

This statement by the Polish Press Bureau was answered by the Czechoslovak Press Bureau on 9th November, 1935, by a statement in which the false Polish view was refuted, substantially in the following terms: When Poland asserts that Czechoslovakia does not fulfil her obligations to the Polish minority, and when on the other hand Czechoslovakia contends that she does fulfil those obligations, and that it is actually Poland that is guilty of a breach of her duty to the Czech and Slovak minorities, these are precisely the "conflicts of opinion," and the "disputes" which fall within the treaties that provide for their settlement by a parity commission and court of arbitration. The Polish standpoint therefore means that Poland refuses to carry out a treaty which she has signed, violating it first of all on the formal side by refusing to apply it in disputes to meet which it was signed. Every State is able to appeal to the international forum to determine who is keeping the terms of a treaty. Czechoslovakia has hitherto preferred that this should be done by mutual agreement. She is convinced, however, that in any case all these questions will appear before the international forum and also acts accordingly. This is the best proof of her sincerity and her good will.

Since then nothing substantially new has occurred in Czechoslovakia's relations with Poland, and therefore we are awaiting Poland's final answer.

Our relations with Austria I have mentioned already in speaking of economic rapprochement in Central Europe and of the standpoint of the Little Entente to Central European problems. I would only like to add briefly that the Little Entente adopted a common standpoint towards the Austrian conscription law, and that the representatives of the Little Entente jointly protested in Vienna in this matter.

Although we cannot regard the explanation of the actual sense of this law given to us by the Austrian Government as fully satisfying, we continue to hope that it will be possible to find the way to a satisfactory and friendly settlement of this matter.

Our relations with Hungary are, on the whole, unchanged. I am glad to note that so far Hungary has not followed the example of Germany and Austria in rejecting the obligations imposed upon her by the peace treaty, and that apparently, she has no intention of doing so. I do not hesitate to hope that with good will on both sides we shall succeed in gradually improving our mutual relations, especially in the economic sphere.

Conclusion

1. Passing to the conclusion of my speech I repeat that two unsettled questions are causing the present disquiet in the international sphere—the problem arising out of the military defeat of Abyssinia and the annexation of that country by Italy, and the problem resulting from the military occupation of the demilitarized Rhine zone by Germany. In both cases it is substantially a conflict provoked by States having violated international obligations, from which it follows that the solution of these matters is of interest to all countries that are concerned for the maintenance of international order and security. It was from this standpoint that the League of Nations intervened in the first-named conflict, and will possibly be called upon in the end to solve also the second problem. Both cases threaten seriously to shatter faith in the stability and possibility of upholding international obligations, as well as confidence in the League of Nations which ought to be the guardian of those obligations.

2. Our attitude towards the two conflicts may be expressed as follows:

In the Italo-Abyssinian dispute we have observed, and continue to observe, neutrality. We took part in the sanctions against Italy as a member of the League of Nations, merely carrying out the decisions, valid and binding upon us, of its organs. We shall also base our further attitude in this matter on the decisions of the League.

In the matter of the demilitarized zone we have stated plainly and openly that Germany's action must be regarded as a breach of international obligations, and that therefore we cannot approve of it.

We await developments and shall very closely follow the further preparatory negotiations between the Great Powers, and if actual negotiations with Germany ensue, we shall participate in them in full accord with the States of the Little Entente, and with our other friends among the Powers.

We are well aware of the gravity of the situation and of the menace to European peace if, within a reasonable space of time a conciliatory settlement of these two questions is not reached, and we therefore express a sincere hope that agreement between the States concerned may be arrived at as soon as possible within the framework of the League of Nations.

In the matter of the suggestions made from various quarters for an alteration in the statutes of the League of Nations I have to remark that we do not regard it as either necessary or expedient to change any of those statutes. We might rather regard it as useful to give some of the provisions of the statutes, of importance for the preservation of peace and the security of States, increased efficacy by the fixing of precise and binding rules for their application. We shall therefore examine with great care every suggestion put forward for a reform of the League of Nations, and agree upon a joint standpoint to such suggestion with the other States of the Little Entente.

3. Although we are not directly interested in any of the questions left open, we none the less follow them with close and careful attention to prevent our interests anywhere being adversely affected. We remain calm for we are conscious of our strength. With allies to lean upon, prepared in the military sphere, and consolidated in the economic sphere we need have no fears for our future. But we must not, of course, pause in our determined and systematic efforts both to increase our own moral and material forces and to strengthen all the guaranties of our external security.

AMERICAN FOREIGN RELATIONS[7]

By the Honorable Cordell Hull
Secretary of State of the United States

Our foreign relations are largely shaped by the physical geography of our country, the characteristics of our people and our historical experience. Those who are in charge of the conduct of foreign policy must suit their actions to these underlying facts with due regard to the shifting circumstances of the times. This is particularly true in a democracy, where even in the short run the policies of the government must rest upon the support of the people.

We inhabit a large country which provides the basis for satisfactory and improving conditions of life. We do not seek or threaten the territory or possessions of others. Great oceans lie between us and the powers of Asia and Europe. Though these are now crossed much more quickly and easily than they used to be, they still enable us to feel somewhat protected against physical impacts from abroad.

We are a numerous, strong, and active people. We have lived and developed in deep traditions of tolerance, of neighborly friendliness, personal freedom, and of self-government. We have had long training in the settlement of differences of opinion and interest among ourselves by discussion and compromise. The winds of doctrine that are blowing so violently in many other lands are moderated here in our democratic atmosphere and tradition.

Our contribution must be in the spirit of our own situation and conceptions. It lies in the willingness to be friends but not allies. We wish extensive and mutually beneficial trade relations. We have the impulse to multiply our personal contacts as shown by the constant American travel abroad. We would share and exchange the gifts which art, the stage, the classroom, and the scientists' and thinkers' study contribute to heighten life and understanding; we have led the world in promoting this sort of interchange among students, teachers, and artists. Our wish that natural human contacts be deeply and fully realized is shown by the great number of international conferences in which we participate, both private and inter-governmental. In such ways we would have our relations grow.

[7] Address delivered in New York on September 15 before the Good Neighbor League.

Failure of Spirit Seen in Outside World

In deciding upon the character of our political relations with the outside world we naturally take into account the conditions prevailing there. These, today, are not tranquil or secure; but on the contrary in many countries are excited and haunted by mutual dread. In less than twenty years events have occurred that have taken away from international agreements their force and reliability as a basis of relations between nations. There appears to have been a great failure of the spirit and out of this has come a many-sided combat of national ambitions, dogmas, and fears.

In many lands the whole national energy has been organized to support absolute aims, far-reaching in character but vaguely defined. These flare like a distant fire in the hills and no one can be sure as to what they mean. There is an increasing acceptance of the idea that the end justifies all means. Under these conditions the individual who questions either means or end is frightened or crushed. For he encounters two controlling rules, compulsory subordination to autocratic will, and the ruthless pressure of might. The result is dread and growing confusion.

Behind this lies the knowledge that laboratories and shops are producing instruments which can blow away human beings as though they were mites in a thunderstorm; and these instruments have been placed in the hands of an increasing number of young men whom their leaders dedicate to the horrors of war. When foreign offices engage in discussion with each other today, they have an inescapable vision of men living in concrete chambers below the earth and concrete and steel forts and tanks upon the earth, and operating destructive machines above the earth. They have strained and striven in many negotiations since the war to dispel that vision, but it appears to grow clearer and clearer.

The world waits. You may be sure that in most human hearts there is the steady murmur of prayer that life need not be yielded up in battle and that there may be peace, at least in our time.

It is in these circumstances we must shape our foreign relations. It is also these circumstances that present to us the problem of seeking to achieve a change in the dominant trend that is so full of menace.

I find as I review the line of foreign policy we have followed, that we come close to Thomas Jefferson's expression—"peace, commerce, and honest friendship with all nations, entangling alliances with none." It is dangerous to take liberties with the great words of a great man, but I would add—settlement of disputes by peaceful means, renunciation of war as an instrument of national policy.

I think that the term "good neighbor" is an apt description of that policy. We have tried to give full meaning to that term. The good neighbor in any community minds his own essential business and does not wilfully disturb the business of others. He mends his fences but does not put up spite fences. He firmly expects that others will not seek to disturb his affairs or dictate to him.

He is tolerant, but his toleration does not include those who would introduce discord from elsewhere. He observes his agreements to the utmost of his ability; he adjusts by friendly methods any troubles that arise; he mingles freely in the give and take of life and concerns himself with the community welfare.

All of this is in contrast with the hermit who isolates himself, who ignores the community, and in his resistance to change, decays in a mean and bitter isolation. But the rôle of the good neighbor is a positive and active one which calls upon the energies, the friendliness, and the self-restraint of man or nation.

Neighborliness of Nations Seen in Fair Dealing

In affairs between nations the neighborliness obviously is less direct than between individuals in the local community. Its expression takes the form of just and fair dealings, without encroachment upon the rights of others, or oppression of the weak or envy of the more fortunate. It contemplates liberal economic relations on the basis of mutual benefit, observance of law and respect for agreements, and reliance upon peaceful processes when controversies arise.

In the everyday work of the Department of State dealing with critical issues, we have resolutely pursued this course.

We have tried to bring together American opinion and opinion in other countries in a common determination against the use of force for the settlement of disputes or for other national purposes. In that connection we have sought to maintain the vitality of the international agreement to renounce war which was signed by virtually all countries of the world when Mr. Kellogg was Secretary of State. But strong nations have chosen to proceed in disregard of that agreement, and this basis for international trust has thus been greatly impaired. We have tried to soften quarrels between other countries when they have arisen.

At times there has been criticism because we would not depart from our traditional policy and join with other governments in collective arrangements carrying the obligation of employing force, if necessary, in case disputes between other countries brought them into war. That responsibility, carrying direct participation in the political relations of the whole of the world outside, we cannot accept, eager as we are to support means for the prevention of war. For current experience indicates how uncertain is the possibility that we, by our action, could vitally influence the policies or activities of other countries from which war might come. It is for the statesmen to continue their effort to effect security by new agreements which will prove more durable than those that have been broken. This government would welcome that achievement. It would be like full light overcoming dense darkness. It is difficult to see how responsible governments can refrain from pushing compromise to its utmost limits to accomplish that result.

Of late we have increased our defense forces substantially. This has appeared essential in the face of the universal increase of armaments elsewhere and the disturbed conditions to which I have alluded. We would not serve the cause of peace by living in the world today without adequate powers of self-defense. We must be sure that in our desire for peace we will not appear to any other country weak and unable to resist the imposition of force or to protect our just rights. At the same time I would make clear with the utmost emphasis that we stand ready to participate in all attempts to limit armaments by mutual accord and await the day when this may be realized.

Canadian Trade Treaty an Index of Friendship

I need say little of our relations with our great neighbor Canada. The American people and the Canadian people have lived in unbroken friendship. A new index of that friendship is the trade agreement signed last year. I have had to reckon with a number of attacks on this or that schedule of the agreement. In virtually every instance I have found, and I do not wish to be partisan in this remark, that the criticism represents misjudgment or distortion of the facts. I have watched the malicious attempts of some to juggle a few minor figures in the trade returns in such a way as to prejudice the minds of particular groups against an agreement which was the first step taken within the last century to enable the American and Canadian peoples to obtain greater mutual benefit from their work and trade.

We have confirmed our good neighbor policy by our actions in dealing with the American republics to the south of us. This administration has made it clear that it would not intervene in any of those republics. It has endorsed this principle by signing at the Montevideo conference the Inter-American Convention on the rights and duties of States; it has abrogated the Platt Amendment contained in our treaty with Cuba; it has withdrawn the American occupying forces from Haiti; it has negotiated new treaties with Panama, which, while fully safeguarding our rights to protect and operate the canal, eliminate the rights we previously possessed to interfere in that republic.

In all this we have shown that we have no wish to dictate to other countries, that we recognize equality of nations and that we believe in the possibility of full cooperation between nations. Later this year there will be held in Argentina a conference between the American republics, which has been warmly welcomed, and there is general confidence that further ways can be found to assure the maintenance of peace on this continent.

Certainly the economic troubles that have pressed so hard on the world during these last few years are one of the main causes of the disturbance of spirit and upset of relations that have taken place. This government has taken the lead in trying to bring about changes in the international trade situation which would improve conditions everywhere.

The needs of our own domestic situation have coincided completely with this undertaking. By 1933 a serious emergency had arisen in our trade relationships with other countries. We had repeatedly increased the barriers to the entry of foreign products into this country, and the sale of American goods abroad was being subjected to increasingly drastic retaliation and restriction on the part of other governments. In addition, we had most substantial investments in foreign countries which our previous policy had thrown into great jeopardy. Many branches of American agriculture and industry required a revival of our trade with other countries if they were to escape continued depression, idleness of resources, and unemployment. The other countries had no smaller need.

Foreign Trade Barriers Lowered by Agreements

Under the authority conferred by the Trade Agreements Act of 1934, we have entered into numerous commercial agreements whereby most carefully selected and limited reductions have been made in our own tariffs. In return, we have secured reductions of the barriers imposed against American goods by other countries and assurance of various kinds against the operation of the trade control systems that have come into existence elsewhere. The vast decline in our foreign trade has ceased. A substantial and steady increase is being recorded. During 1935 our sales abroad exceeded those of 1932, the lowest year, by $671,000,000. The trade records of 1936 to date indicate that this figure will be surpassed. This has been an extremely wholesome factor in the improvement in our own conditions and in building up the world's purchasing power. Our imports of foreign goods have similarly increased, reflecting chiefly the enlarged American demand for raw materials, arising from the improvement of productive activity in the United States and our increased purchasing power.

In the negotiation of these agreements the principle of equality has been maintained in the belief that trade conducted on this basis brings the greatest economic benefit, has the greatest possibilities of expansion, and involves the least conflict. We are vigorously striving to secure similar equality of treatment on the part of other countries with which we have negotiated. In connection with this program we have refused to be drawn into a system of bilateral balancing between pairs of countries because this system is comparatively sterile and requires direct government management of international trade, which soon extends to management of domestic production. At the same time we have been alert to the problem of protecting our trade interests against the incidental disadvantages that we might suffer from the practice of such a system by other countries.

The trade policy this country is pursuing fits well into our domestic economic situation and policies. I am willing to leave this judgment to the arbitration of facts. Certainly by now it should be clear, even to those engaged in industries that have been the most direct beneficiaries of excessive tariffs, that this alone will not bring them prosperity. It should also be apparent that they can thrive only when other branches of production thrive, including those that habitually dispose of a large part of their products in foreign markets.

The rebuilding of international trade offers a splendid opportunity for governments to improve the conditions of their people and to assure them the necessary means of acquiring the essentials of well-being and the raw materials for production. If this result can be achieved, one of the fertile causes of dissension and possible war would be weakened or removed. The plans and hopes of millions of individuals now appear to have no place except in military formation. An improvement of economic conditions would guarantee another place. Advancement in this direction need not await a solution of all political difficulties. Terms have been found by which advance can be made even in the face of the monetary uncertainty which still exists. A great opportunity awaits great leadership.

In trade interchange baleful elements enter particularly the trade in arms, ammunition, and implements of war. This trade is at present mainly incidental to the preparation for war. However, in some times and circumstances, it may itself be an element in stimulating or provoking war. Therefore, we have established a system requiring full disclosure regarding American trade in this field by placing those engaged in it under a license plan. Whether and to what extent it may be wise to regulate or restrict such trade between ourselves and other nations, for reasons other than the protection of military secrets, is a matter on which we are constantly weighing our current experience. Our existing legal authority is limited. But, as in the present Spanish situation, we assert our influence to the utmost to prevent arms shipped from this country from thwarting national or international efforts to maintain peace or end conflict. But action of that character cannot best be governed by inflexible rule, for, to a large extent, it must be determined in the light of the facts and circumstances of each situation. This much is certain—we are always ready to discourage to the utmost the traffic in arms when required in the interest of peace.

Must Be Ready for Stand in Case of New War

Up to this point I have dealt with the principles of our policies and relationships with other countries when peace prevails. Lately, after a lapse of almost twenty years, we have been called upon to consider with great seriousness the question of what these relationships should be if war were unhappily to occur again among the other great countries of the world. We must squarely face the fact that to stay clear of a widespread major war will require great vigilance, poise and careful judgment in dealing with such interferences with our peaceful rights and activities as may take place.

Legislation recently passed provides some of the main essentials in a wise anticipatory policy. I have in mind the resolutions of Congress of 1935 and 1936 which, in addition to providing for the licensing of all imports and exports of arms, ammunition, and implements of war, prohibit their shipment to belligerent nations. Those same resolutions prohibit the flotation of loans and the establishment of credits in our market by belligerent countries and otherwise strengthen our existing neutrality laws. On some of these matters the Congress by law has modified policies formerly pursued by this government in times of war abroad. There are other vital aspects of this problem which will continue to receive the careful attention and study of the Department of State.

The problems arising during a period of neutrality are so great that they constantly renew in one the determination to spare no reasonable effort to play a full part in the encouragement of the maintenance of peace. We have sought to demonstrate that we are interested in peace everywhere. Surely this endeavor must continue to command our full abilities if war elsewhere can create such difficulties for us, if it can change for the worse the world in which we must live, if it can threaten the civilization with which all of us are concerned.

I cannot believe that the world has completely changed in mentality and desire since those great decades when the principles of liberty and democracy were extending their reign. I believe that this was a natural evolution of our civilization. I do not believe that with the great and growing facilities for education and for personal development people will permanently abandon their individual liberties and political rights. In my judgment it is not a basic defect of democratic institutions that has led to their decline in so many places, but rather the onset of weariness, fear, and indifference, which can and must be dispelled. These are the heritage of the last war. They must not be permitted to bring on another.

Let me return to a remark that I made in the beginning—that the direction of our foreign policy must be acceptable to the people. Our task is to formulate out of the wishes and wisdom of a popular democracy a sound foreign policy which will insure peace and favor progress and prosperity. We must be on guard against the hasty, excited impulse, the quick upsurge of passing emotion.

Satisfactory foreign policy must be able to count upon the qualities of patience, of sympathetic understanding, of steady poise and of assured inner strength among the people. In the past crises of our history Americans have shown that they possess these qualities in full measure. I do not doubt that they are still present as a firm support. Against the walls of our democratic methods and institutions storms from elsewhere beat violently. Let us avoid flabbiness of spirit, weakness of body, grave dissent within our own numbers, and we shall have nothing to fear from these storms. We must keep before us the knowledge that our democracy was builded on the solid qualities of hardihood, individual self-reliance, full willingness to put general welfare above personal interest in any great matter of national interest, forebearance in every direction and abiding patriotism. They alone can furnish the necessary assurance that our foreign policy and our foreign relations will continue to bring peace with the whole world and will not fail in that leadership appropriate to a country as great as ours.

FRANCE FAITHFUL TO DEMOCRACY[a]

By Léon Blum, Premier of France

In the present anxiety of European opinion and on the eve of the Geneva Assembly, the Government of the French Republic believes it opportune to recall, in terms simple and clear, on what constant doctrine her political acts are founded.

By an immense majority, France remains attached, with thoughtful passion, to the memories and traditions of the French Revolution.

France believes in political liberty. She believes in civic equality. She believes in human fraternity. She professes that all citizens are born free and equal before the law. Among the fundamental rights of the individual she places liberty of thought and conscience in the first rank.

She considers that action of the State has for its essential object to introduce application of these principles more and more profoundly into legal institutions, into social understandings, and into international relations. It is in this sense that the French State is a democratic State and that the French nation believes in democracy.

Is this doctrine weakened by what is called today "realism," that is to say, by the utilitarian consideration of facts? Certainly not. Experience has not undone the belief of the French mind.

The principles evolved by the revolution of 1789 have spread over the entire world. They have changed the moral aspect of the universe. They have slowly eliminated the struggles between races and religions that bled Europe for centuries and were thought to have been eliminated forever.

Miseries Are Alleviated

They have transported onto the plane of pure thought or the terrain of constructive action the eternal quarrel of doctrines. They have brought forth unheard-of expansion in science and culture, while limiting the miseries engendered by industrialization.

Those who condemn them often unknowingly profit from them. Without the civil liberty that the French Revolution proclaimed, the authoritarian States of Europe would not today have at their heads men risen from the depths of the people and drawing from that origin their titles and their pride.

[a] Radio broadcast, Paris, September 17, 1936.

Stability has been spoken of. The history of the last century has demonstrated that democratic régimes offered at least as much stability as governmental systems founded on the all-powerfulness of one man, even though that all-powerfulness be explained by genius.

Order, which is indispensable to all collective organization, has been spoken of. Democracy is precisely the régime that permits societies to progress in order, since it makes progress depend on the general will and on a more and more enlightened will.

France can cite her own example. For three months the government has been carrying out important social reforms. It has done so with the widest popular movement of expectation and hope. But it has done so without a single clash between citizens, without order having been disturbed in the street a single time, without a single institution having been overthrown, without a single citizen having been despoiled. It will be so tomorrow and it was so yesterday.

Democracy Rests on Order

Democracy, which rests upon order and which imposes order upon the thoughtful will of the greatest number, is contrary to anarchy. In any case, how can the magnificent testimony offered for so many years by the great Anglo-Saxon nations be rejected?

Is it not thanks to democracy that Britain has been able to control that continuous and almost insensible adaptation between progress and tradition which has permitted her to transform all her institutions while remaining faithful to herself? Is it not thanks to democracy that the United States has been able to bring about a prodigious economic renewal in a few years without compromising legal order for a single instant, without going outside the framework of the Constitution elaborated just after the War of Independence by American disciples of Montesquieu and Rousseau?

No, democracy does not emerge condemned by the long trial waged against it. It is justified by proof as by reason. The debt that humanity has contracted toward it during 150 years is infinite. France knows it and France remains faithful to democracy.

Propaganda Not Desired

Although she keeps her full confidence in the age-old power to spread her influence, France does not claim to impose on any people the principles of government that she believes wisest and justest. She respects their sovereignty as she expects them to respect hers.

France rejects utterly the idea of wars of propaganda and wars of reprisal. The causes of war that weigh on the world are already heavy enough without her wanting to add to them with a doctrinal crusade, even for ideas that she believes right and just, even against systems that she believes false and evil.

She wants to live in peace with all the nations of the world, whatever may be their internal régime. She seeks, in harmony with all nations in the world, to reduce the causes of conflict from which one day war may spring. With all, whoever they may be, provided only they desire peace, she will seek its organization and its consideration. There is not a single contact, not a single interview, not a single discussion that she will refuse.

At the same time, as there is a democratic and humane conception of government, there is also a democratic and humane conception of peace. It is to that conception that the French nation remains attached. It is that conception which the French Government will seek to have accepted.

Self-Determination Upheld

That French peace supposes for all nations liberty for self-determination. It supposes equality of right between States, big or little, as between individuals. It supposes fraternity, that is to say, progressive elimination of war, solidarity against an aggressor, and material and moral disarmament.

It is because the League of Nations is itself founded on these principles that the international action of France is founded on the League. It seeks to strengthen the links between the nations that meet at Geneva to assure to the covenant she has signed more and more force and effectiveness. It seeks to organize mutual assistance. It seeks to halt the armaments race, and this country will not cease to repeat her appeal until she has been heard.

It seeks for reconciliation, for reciprocal understanding, for collaboration between all peoples, and men who speak in the name of the French nation can make this claim: That there has never passed their lips any word animated by a different spirit.

This conception of peace derives from democratic doctrine, but it holds its own against attacks of realism, for experience has proved it. History shows that no real, stable peace can be established on injustice or on egoism. Any sincere observer who looks at the present state of the world must be convinced that the only stable peace is a general peace—that only viable solutions of European problems are all-round settlements.

Peace Must Be General

Peace must be general because war would be general, because there is not a single armed conflict in present Europe that could be limited or bounded. It is this conviction that the government expresses when it speaks of collective security and indivisible peace. It is this conviction that it links with the sentiment of honor when it affirms its fidelity to the engagements taken to signed contracts and to concluded pacts, and when it manifests at the same time its firm intention to extend them right up to the universal organization of peoples united by peace in a common prosperity.

This will for peace is for the French nation a unanimous sentiment. There exist in France undoubtedly civil divisions. It is not liberty that engenders them, for they result from oppositions of thought and antagonisms of interest. But liberty permits their expression. It permits also an element of life and progress to be derived from their free play. There are in France doctrines and parties that oppose each other. In them France sees the principle of force and not of feebleness.

But just as she is unanimous in her will for peace, she would be unanimous tomorrow, as in every hour of her history, if preservation of the security of the fatherland or even more if defense of her soil were in question. She would be unanimous for maintenance of her complete independence of conduct, her full liberty of decision and of choice against any pressure or any interdiction.

She seeks to constrain no one. She will not permit herself to be constrained by any one, directly or indirectly.

She demands that there be always wisdom in her strength, but that there be always pride in her will for peace.

It is in this spirit that she intends to enter upon the international discussions that are about to open. That is the new contribution which, after so many others, old and recent, she desires to bring to the essential work of peace, awaited by the peoples of the world in anguish and in hope.

LIST OF PUBLICATIONS

These documents present the views of distinguished leaders of opinion of many countries on vital international problems and reproduce the texts of official treaties, diplomatic correspondence, and draft plans for international projects such as the Permanent Court of International Justice. *International Conciliation* appeared under the imprint of the American Association for International Conciliation, No. 1, April, 1907, to No. 199, June, 1924. The most recent publications are listed below. A complete list will be sent upon application to International Conciliation, 405 West 117th Street, New York City.

311. Restoration of International Trade: Text of Radio Address delivered by the Honorable Cordell Hull on March 23, 1935; American Trade Policy and World Recovery, by Peter Molyneaux; Program of the International Economic Conference held at Chatham House, London, March 5-7, 1935.
June, 1935.

312. Neutrality and War Prevention, by Henry L. Stimson; The Neutrality of the Good Neighbor, by James Brown Scott; Speech of Sir Samuel Hoare in British House of Commons, July 11, 1935; British Foreign Policy (London *Times*, Editorial, July 12, 1935).
September, 1935.

313. The Sanctity of Treaties, by John B. Whitton, Associate Professor of International Law, Princeton University. The Price of Peace, by Stephen Gwynn, President of the Irish Literary Society.
October, 1935.

314. Italy and Ethiopia. Abyssinia: The Background of the Conflict, by a group of expert students of international affairs; The Threat of War and the Pact of Paris (statement to the press, September 12, 1935), by the Honorable Cordell Hull; Collective Action for Security Demanded (address before League Assembly, September 11, 1935), by Sir Samuel Hoare; Text of Broadcast by Sir Samuel Hoare, October 15, 1935; France Faithful to League Covenant (address before League Assembly, September 13, 1935), by M. Pierre Laval; Abstract of the Report on Italy's Aggressions, adopted by the Council of the League of Nations, October 7, 1935.
November, 1935.

315. Andrew Carnegie, Benefactor, by Nicholas Murray Butler. Sanctions in the Italo-Ethiopian Conflict, by an expert on International Affairs; Italy's Conflict with Ethiopia, by His Excellency Dr. Augusto Rosso; Report on Italo-Ethiopian Dispute adopted by League Council under Article 15, Paragraph 4, of the Covenant on October 7, 1935; Co-ordination of Measures under Article 16 of the Covenant (Proposals adopted by the Co-ordination Committee of the League, October 11-19, 1935).
December, 1935.

316. A Study of Neutrality Legislation: Report of a Committee of the National Peace Conference, with an Introduction by James T. Shotwell.
January, 1936.

317. The Present Status of the League of Nations, by N. D. Houghton, Professor of Political Science at the University of Arizona. Text of Resignation as High Commissioner for Refugees Coming from Germany, by James G. McDonald.
February, 1936.

318. The Fallacy of Conquest, by Nathaniel Peffer. International Peace, by Thomas John Watson. Text of the Constitution of the Philippines.
March, 1936.

319. Germany and Japan Today: Hitler's Treaty Repudiation; Franco-Soviet Treaty of Mutual Assistance; Japan's Political Murderers, by K. K. Kawakami; The Japanese-American War Myth, by Vernon Nash.
April, 1936.

320. The Chaco Arms Embargo, by Manley O. Hudson. Text of Peace Plan Communicated to the Locarno Powers by the French Government on April 8, 1936. Insurance against War, by William E. Richardson. Facing the Future, by Mrs. August Belmont. Isolation, by J. N. Métaxa.
May, 1936.

321. The United States and World Organization during 1935.
June, 1936.

322. British Foreign Policy: Debate in the House of Commons, June 18 and 23, 1936. French Foreign Policy: Text of Government's Declaration to Parliament, June 23, 1936. American Foreign Policy: Text of President Roosevelt's Address at Chautauqua, New York, August 14, 1936.
September, 1936.

323. American Foreign Trade Policies, by Cordell Hull. The Consequences of Economic Nationalism, by Lionel Robbins. World Police for World Peace, by Viscount Allenby. The Responsibility of Governments and Peoples, by Cordell Hull. Europe at the Crossroads, by Kamil Krofta. American Foreign Relations, by Cordell Hull. France Faithful to Democracy, by Léon Blum.
October, 1936.